Big Data Analytics

Big Data Analytics

From Strategic Planning to Enterprise Integration with Tools, Techniques, NoSQL, and Graph

David Loshin

AMSTERDAM • BOSTON • HEIDELBERG • LONDON
NEW YORK • OXFORD • PARIS • SAN DIEGO
SAN FRANCISCO • SINGAPORE • SYDNEY • TOKYO
Morgan Kaufmann is an imprint of Elsevier

Morgan Kaufmann is an imprint of Elsevier
225 Wyman Street, Waltham, MA 02451, USA

Notices
Knowledge and best practice in this field are constantly changing. As new research and experience broaden our understanding, changes in research methods or professional practices, may become necessary.

Practitioners and researchers must always rely on their own experience and knowledge in evaluating and using any information or methods described herein. In using such information or methods they should be mindful of their own safety and the safety of others, including parties for whom they have a professional responsibility.

To the fullest extent of the law, neither the Publisher nor the authors, contributors, or editors, assume any liability for any injury and/or damage to persons or property as a matter of products liability, negligence or otherwise, or from any use or operation of any methods, products, instructions, or ideas contained in the material herein.

Library of Congress Cataloging-in-Publication Data
A catalog record for this book is available from the Library of Congress

British Library Cataloguing-in-Publication Data
A catalogue record for this book is available from the British Library

ISBN: 978-0-12-417319-4

For information on all MK publications
visit our website at *www.mkp.com*

This book has been manufactured using Print On Demand technology. Each copy is produced to order and is limited to black ink. The online version of this book will show color figures where appropriate.

ELSEVIER   **Book Aid** International   Working together to grow libraries in developing countries

www.elsevier.com • www.bookaid.org

CONTENTS

FOREWORD

In the summer of 1995, I attended my first conference for information technology professionals. The event, called Interex, was an annual convention for users of the HP 3000, Hewlett-Packard's midrange business computer system known at the time for its reliability—and a devoted user base. More than 10,000 of these users gathered in Toronto that August to swap tips and pester HP executives for information about the future of their beloved system.

After spending several days talking with these IT managers, I came away with two observations:

1. The managers were grappling with rising technology demands from business executives and office workers who wanted more out of their IT investments.
2. While everyone in the Toronto Convention Center was talking about the HP 3000, there was a 100-foot-tall "WINDOWS '95" banner hanging from the nearby CN Tower, a prominent landmark in the city's skyline.

That banner was not part of the Interex event. But it would not be long before Microsoft's new desktop operating system would influence the work of just about everyone who used a PC.

It has always been this way. Innovations in computer hardware, communications technology, and software development regularly enter to challenge IT professionals to adapt to new opportunities and associated challenges. The latest edition of this recurrent dynamic is big data analytics, which takes advantage of advances in software programming, open source code, and commodity hardware to promise major gains in our ability to collect and analyze vast amounts of data—and new kinds of data—for fresh insights. The kinds of techniques that allow Google to index the Web, Facebook to build social graphs, and Netflix to recommend movies can be applied to functions like marketing (what's the next best offer for Marjorie?), risk management (the storm is tracking near our warehouse, better move the goods today), and equipment maintenance (the sensor says it's time to replace that engine part).

Those possibilities and many others have generated much interest. Venture capital is flowing to startups as database architects are cool again. Leaders in health care, finance, insurance, and other industries are racing to hire talented "data scientists" to develop algorithms to discover competitive advantages. Universities are launching master's programs in analytics in response to corporate demands and a projected skills gap. Statisticians are joining celebrity ranks, with one sparking cable news debates about presidential election predictions and another starring in TED Talk videos on data visualization design.

There is so much going on, in fact, that a busy IT professional looking for relevant help could use a personal guide to explain the issues in a style that acknowledges some important conditions about their world: They likely have a full list of ongoing projects. Their organization has well-defined IT management practices. They stipulate that adopting new technologies is not easy.

This is the kind of book you are reading now. David Loshin, an experienced IT consultant and author, is adept at explaining how technologies work and why they matter, without technical or marketing jargon. He has years of practice both posing and answering questions about data management, data warehousing, business intelligence, and analytics.

I know this because I have asked him. I first met David in 2012 at an online event he moderated to explain issues involved in making big data analytics work in business. I sought him out to discuss the issues in more detail as the editor of *Data Informed* (http://data-informed.com/) an online publication that chronicles these trends and shares best practices for IT and business professionals. Those early conversations led to David writing a series of articles for *Data Informed* that forms the basis for this book, on issues ranging from the market and business drivers for big data analytics, to use cases for these emerging technologies, to strategies for assessing their relevance to your organization.

Along the way, David and I have found ourselves agreeing about a key lesson from his years of working in IT (or, in my case, reporting on it): New big data analytics technologies are exciting, and represent a great opportunity. But making any new technology work effectively requires understanding the tools you need, having the right people working together on common goals, and establishing the right business processes to create value from the work.

The teachings in this book go beyond this straightforward three-legged stool of technologies–skills–processes. At the end of each chapter, there are "thought exercises" that challenge you to consider the technology, business, and management concepts in the context of your organization. This is where David provides you the opportunity to answer the kinds of questions that will help you evaluate next steps for making the technologies covered here valuable to you.

These are like signposts to direct your work in adapting to the big data analytics field. It's much better than a 10-story banner blaring to a city that your world is about to change. Here, the signs come with full explanations and advice about how to make that change work for you.

Michael Goldberg

PREFACE

INTRODUCTION

In technology, it seems, what comes around goes around. At least in my experience, it certainly seems that way. Over recent times, the concepts of "big data" and "big data analytics" have become ubiquitous—it is heard to visit a web site, open a newspaper, or read a magazine that does not refer to one or both of those phrases. Yet the technologies that are incorporated into big data—massive parallelism, huge data volumes, data distribution, high-speed networks, high-performance computing, task and thread management, and data mining and analytics—are not new.

During the first phase of my career in the late 1980s and early 1990s I was a software developer for a company building programming language compilers for supercomputers. Most of these high-end systems were multiprocessor systems, employed massive parallelism, and were driven by (by the standards of the times, albeit) large data sets. My specific role was looking at code optimization, particularly focusing on increasing data bandwidth to the processors and taking advantage of the memory hierarchies upon which these systems were designed and implemented. And interestingly, much of the architectures and techniques used for designing hardware and developing software were not new either—much credit goes to early supercomputers such as the Illiac IV, the first massively parallel computing system that was developed in the early 1970s.

That is why the big data phenomenon is so fascinating to me: not the appearance of new technology, but rather how known technology finally comes into the mainstream. When the details of technology that was bleeding edge 20 years ago appear regularly in The New York Times, The Wall Street Journal, and The Economist, you know it has finally arrived.

THE CHALLENGE OF ADOPTING NEW TECHNOLOGY

Many people have a natural affinity to new technology—there is often the perception that the latest and shiniest silver bullet will not only eliminate all the existing problems in the organization will but also lead to the minting of a solid stream of gold coins enriching the entire organization. And in those organizations that are not leading the revolution to adoption, there is the lingering fear of abandonment—if they don't adopt the technology they will be left far behind, even if there is no clear value proposition for it in the first place.

Clearly, it would be unwise to commit to a new technology without assessing the components of its value—expected value driver "lift," as compared to the total cost of operations. Essentially, testing and piloting new technology is necessary to maintain competitiveness and ensure technical feasibility. But in many organizations, the processes to expeditiously mainstream new techniques and tools often bypass existing program governance and corporate best practices. The result is that pilot projects are prematurely moved into "production" are really just point solutions relying on islands of data that don't scale from the performance perspective nor fit into the enterprise from an architectural perspective.

WHAT THIS BOOK IS

The goal of this book is to provide a firm grounding in laying out a strategy for adopting big data techniques. It is meant to provide an overview of what big data is and why it can add value, what types of problems are suited to a big data approach, and how to properly plan to determine the need, align the right people in the organization, and develop a strategic plan for integration.

On the other hand, this book is not meant as a "how-to" for big data application development, MapReduce programming, or implementing Hadoop. Rather, my intent is to provide an overview within each chapter that addresses some pertinent aspect of the ecosystem or the process of adopting big data:

- Chapter 1: We consider the market conditions that have enabled broad acceptance of big data analytics, including commoditization of hardware and software, increased data volumes, growing variation in types of data assets for analysis, different methods for data delivery, and increased expectations for real-time integration of analytical results into operational processes.

- Chapter 2: In this chapter, we look at the characteristics of business problems that traditionally have required resources that exceeded the enterprises' scopes, yet are suited to solutions that can take advantage of the big data platforms (either dedicated hardware or virtualized/cloud based).
- Chapter 3: Who in the organization needs to be involved in the process of acquiring, proving, and deploying big data solutions? And what are their roles and responsibilities? This chapter looks at the adoption of new technology and how the organization must align to integrate into the system development life cycle.
- Chapter 4: This chapter expands on the previous one by looking at some key issues that often plague new technology adoption and show that the key issues are not new ones and that there is likely to be organizational knowledge that can help in fleshing out a reasonable strategic plan.
- Chapter 5: In this chapter, we look at the need for oversight and governance for the data, especially when those developing big data applications often bypass traditional IT and data management channels.
- Chapter 6: In this chapter, we look at specialty-hardware designed for analytics and how they are engineered to accommodate large data sets.
- Chapter 7: This chapter discusses and provides a high-level overview of tool suites such as Hadoop.
- Chapter 8: This chapter examines the MapReduce programming model.
- Chapter 9: In this chapter, we look at a variety of alternative methods of data management methods that are being adopted for big data application development.
- Chapter 10: This chapter looks at business problems suited for graph analytics, what differentiates the problems from traditional approaches and considerations for discovery versus search analyses.
- Chapter 11: This short final chapter reviews best practices for incrementally adopting big data into the enterprise.

WHY YOU SHOULD BE READING THIS BOOK

You have probably picked up this book for one or more of these very good reasons:

- You are a senior manager seeking to take advantage of your organization's information to create or add to corporate value by increasing revenue, decreasing costs, improving productivity, mitigating risks, or improving the customer experience.
- You are the Chief Information Officer or Chief Data Officer of an organization who desires to make the best use of the enterprise information asset.
- You are a manager who has been asked to develop a big data program.
- You are a manager who has been asked to take over a floundering big data application.
- You are a manager who has been asked to take over a successful big data program.
- You are a senior business executive who wants to explore the value that big data can add to your organization.
- You are a business staff member who desires more insight into the way that your organization does business.
- You are a database or software engineer who has been appointed a technical manager for a big data program.
- You are a software engineer who aspires to be the manager of a big data program.
- You are an analyst of engineer working on a big data framework who aspires to replace your current manager.
- You are a business analyst who has been asked to join a big data application team.
- You are a senior manager and your directly reporting managers have started talking about big data using terminology you think they expect you to understand.
- You are a middle-level manager or engineer and your manager has started talking about big data using terminology you think they expect you to understand.
- You are just interested in nig.

How do I know so much about you? Because at many times in my life, I *was* you—either working on or managing a project for which I had some knowledge gaps, for an organization full of people not sure of why they were doing, what they were doing, with very few clear success criteria or performance metrics. At times I would have loved to have had a straightforward book to consult for a quick lookup or a more in-depth read, without having to spend a huge amount of money on a technical book that only briefly addressed a topic of interest. And even more acutely, it is good to have an unbiased text to help differentiate marketing hype from reality.

OUR APPROACH TO KNOWLEDGE TRANSFER

As I have mentioned in the prefaces to my recent books ("Business Intelligence—The Savvy Manager's Guide, Second Edition," "Master Data Management," and "The Practitioner's Guide to Data Quality Improvement") I remain devoted to helping organizations strategically improve their capabilities in gaining the best advantage from what might be called "information utility." My prior experiences in failed data management activities drove me to quit my last "real job" (as I like to say) and start my own consulting practice to prove that there are better ways to organize and plan information-oriented program.

My company, Knowledge Integrity Inc. (www.knowledge-integrity. com), was developed to help organizations form successful high-performance computing, business intelligence, analytics, information quality, data governance, and master data management programs. As a way of distinguishing my effort from other consulting companies, I also instituted a few important corporate rules about the way we would do business:

1. Our mission was to develop and popularize methods for enterprise data management and utility. As opposed to the craze for patenting technology, methods, and processes, we would openly publish our ideas so as to benefit anyone willing to invest the time and energy to internalize the ideas we were promoting.
2. We would encourage clients to adopt our methods within their success patterns. It is a challenge (and perhaps in a way, insulting) to walk into an organization and tell people who have done their jobs successfully that they need to drop what they are doing and change every aspect of the way they work. We believe that every organization has its own methods for success, and our job is to craft a way to integrate performance-based information quality management into the existing organizational success structure.

3. We would not establish ourselves as permanent fixtures. We believe that information management is a core competency that should be managed within the organization, and our goal for each engagement is to establish the fundamental aspects of the program, transfer technology to internal resources, and then be on our way. I often say that if we do our job right, we work ourselves out of a contract.
4. We are not "selling a product," we are engaged to solve customer problems. We are less concerned about rigid compliance to a trademarked methodology than we are about making sure that the customer's core issues are resolved, and if that means adapting our methods to the organization's that is the most appropriate way to get things done. I also like to say that we are successful when the client comes up with our ideas.
5. Effective communication is the key to change management. Articulating how good information management techniques enhance organizational effectiveness and performance is the first step in engaging business clients and ensuring their support and sponsorship. We would invest part of every engagement in establishing a strong business case accompanied by collateral information that can be socialized within and across the enterprise.

With these rules in mind, our first effort was to consolidate our ideas for semantic, rule-oriented data quality management in a book, "Enterprise Knowledge Management—The Data Quality Approach," which was published in 2001 by Morgan Kaufmann. I have been told by a number of readers that the book is critical in their development of a data quality management program, and the new technical ideas proposed for rule-based data quality monitoring have, in the intervening years, been integrated into all of the major data quality vendor product suites.

Since 1999, we have developed a graduate-level course on data quality for New York University, multiple day-courses for The Data Warehousing Institute (www.tdwi.org), presented numerous sessions at conferences and chapter meetings for DAMA (the Data Management Association), course and online content for DATAVERSITY (www.dataversity.net), provided columns for Robert Seiner's Data Administration Newsletter (www.tdan.com), monthly columns for DM Review (www.dmreview.com), a downloadable course on data quality from Better Management (www.bettermanagement.com), and hosting an expert channel and monthly newsletter at the Business Intelligence Network (www.b-eye-network.com) and TechTarget (www. TechTarget.com).

We are frequently asked by vendors across the spectrum to provide analysis and thought leadership in many areas of data management. We have consulted in the public sector for both federal, state, and other global government agencies. We have guided data management projects in a number of industries, including government, financial services, health care, manufacturing, energy services, insurance, and social services, among others.

Since we started the company, the awareness of the value of information management has been revealed to be one of the most important topics that senior management faces. In practices that have emerged involving the exploitation of enterprise data, such as Enterprise Resource Planning (ERP), Supply Chain Management (SCM), and Customer Relationship Management (CRM), there is a need for a consolidated view of high-quality data representing critical views of business information. Increased regulatory oversight, increased need for information exchange, business performance management, and the value of service-oriented architecture are driving a greater focus on performance-oriented management of enterprise data with respect to utility: accessibility, consistency, currency, freshness, and usability of a common information asset.

CONTACT ME

While my intention is that this book will provide a guide to a strategic plan for big data, there are situations where some expert advice helps get the ball rolling. The practices and approaches described in this book are abstracted from numerous real client engagements, and our broad experience may be able to jump-start your mission for deploying a big data application. In the spirit of openness, I am always happy to answer questions, provide some additional details, and hear feedback about the approaches that I have put in this book and that Knowledge Integrity has employed successfully with our clients since 1999.

We are always looking for opportunities to help organizations establish the value proposition, develop the blueprint, roadmaps, and program plan, and help in implementing the business intelligence and information utilization strategy, and would welcome any opportunities to share ideas and seek out ways we can help your organization. I mean it, I really want to hear from you.

I can be reached via my e-mail address, loshin@knowledge-integrity.com, or through Knowledge Integrity's company web site, www.knowledge-integrity.com, via www.davidloshin.info, or through the web site I have set up for this book, www.bigdataliteracy.com.

David Loshin

ACKNOWLEDGMENTS

What is presented in this book is a culmination of years of experience in projects and programs associated with best practices in employing data management tools, techniques, processes, and working with people. A number of people were key contributors to the development of this book, and I take this opportunity to thank them for their support.

First of all, my wonderful wife Jill deserves the most credit for perseverance and for her encouragement in completing the book. I also must thank my children, Kira, Jonah, Brianna, Gabriella, and Emma, for their help as well.

Much of the material in this book has been adapted from a series of articles that I wrote for a great web site, www.data-informed.com. Editor Michael Goldberg and publisher Michael Nadeau were instrumental in motivating, editing, and enabling the publication of this book.

Abie Reifer has provided insight, guidance, and suggestions for improving the content.

Critical parts of this book were inspired by works that I was commissioned to assemble for vendors in the big data space such as HP/Vertica, SAP/Sybase, ParAccel/Pervasive, Teradata, and YarcData, as well as material presented through my expert channel at www.b-eye-network. com, adapted from presentation material at conferences hosted by Wilshire Conferences, DATAVERSITY, DebTech International, The Data Warehousing Institute (www.tdwi.org), and vendor-hosted webinars and live events.

CHAPTER 1

Market and Business Drivers for Big Data Analytics

1.1 SEPARATING THE BIG DATA REALITY FROM HYPE

There are few technology phenomena that have taken both the technical and the mainstream media by storm than "big data." From the analyst communities to the front pages of the most respected sources of journalism, the world seems to be awash in big data projects, activities, analyses, and so on. However, as with many technology fads, there is some murkiness in its definition, which lends to confusion, uncertainty, and doubt when attempting to understand how the methodologies can benefit the organization.

Therefore, it is best to begin with a definition of big data. The analyst firm Gartner can be credited with the most-frequently used (and perhaps, somewhat abused) definition:

> Big data *is high-volume, high-velocity and high-variety information assets that demand cost-effective, innovative forms of information processing for enhanced insight and decision making.*[1]

For the most part, in popularizing the big data concept, the analyst community and the media have seemed to latch onto the alliteration that appears at the beginning of the definition, hyperfocusing on what is referred to as the "3 Vs—volume, velocity, and variety." Others have built upon that meme to inject additional Vs such as "value" or "variability," intended to capitalize on an apparent improvement to the definition.

The ubiquity of the Vs definition notwithstanding, it is worth noting that the origin of the concept is not new, but was provided by (at the time Meta Group, now Gartner) analyst Doug Laney in a research note from 2001 about "3-D Data Management," in which he noted:

---

[1]Gartner's IT Glossary. Accessed from <http://www.gartner.com/it-glossary/big-data/> (Last accessed 08-08-13).

While enterprises struggle to consolidate systems and collapse redundant databases to enable greater operational, analytical, and collaborative consistencies, changing economic conditions have made this job more difficult. E-commerce, in particular, has exploded data management challenges along three dimensions: volumes, velocity and variety. In 2001/02, IT organizations must compile a variety of approaches to have at their disposal for dealing with each.[2]

The challenge with Gartner's definition is twofold. First, the impact of truncating the definition to concentrate on the Vs effectively distils out two other critical components of the message:

1. "cost-effective innovative forms of information processing" (the means by which the benefit can be achieved);
2. "enhanced insight and decision-making" (the desired outcome).

The second is a bit subtler: the definition is not really a definition, but rather a description. People in an organization cannot use the definition to determine whether they are using big data solutions or even if they have problems that need a big data solution. The same issue impedes the ability to convey a value proposition because of the difficulty in scoping what is intended to be designed, developed, and delivered and what the result really means to the organization.

Basically, it is necessary to look beyond what is essentially a marketing definition to understand the concept's core intent as the first step in evaluating the value proposition. Big data is fundamentally about applying innovative and cost-effective techniques for solving existing and future business problems whose resource requirements (for data management space, computation resources, or immediate, in-memory representation needs) exceed the capabilities of traditional computing environments as currently configured within the enterprise. Another way of envisioning this is shown in Figure 1.1.

To best understand the value that big data can bring to your organization, it is worth considering the market conditions that have enabled its apparently growing acceptance as a viable option to supplement the intertwining of operational and analytical business application in light of exploding data volumes. Over the course of this book, we hope to

[2]Doug Laney. Deja VVVu: others claiming Gartner's construct for big data, January 2012. Accessed from <http://blogs.gartner.com/doug-laney/deja-vvvue-others-claiming-gartners-volume-velocity-variety-construct-for-big-data/>.

Figure 1.1 Cracking the big data nut.

quantify some of the variables that are relevant in evaluating and making decisions about integrating big data as part of an enterprise information management architecture, focusing on topics such as:

- characterizing what is meant by "massive" data volumes;
- reviewing the relationship between the speed of data creation and delivery and the integration of analytics into real-time business processes;
- exploring reasons that the traditional data management framework cannot deal with owing to growing data variability;
- qualifying the quantifiable measures of value to the business;
- developing a strategic plan for integration;
- evaluating the technologies;
- designing, developing, and moving new applications into production.

Qualifying the business value is particularly important, especially when the forward-looking stakeholders in an organization need to effectively communicate the business value of embracing big data platforms, and correspondingly, big data analytics. For example, a business justification might show how incorporating a new analytics framework can be a competitive differentiator. Companies that develop customer upselling profiles based on limited data sampling face a disadvantage when compared to enterprises that create comprehensive customer models encompassing *all* the data about the customer intended to increase revenues while enhancing the customer experience.

Adopting a technology as a knee-jerk reaction to media buzz has a lowered chance of success than assessing how that technology can be leveraged along with the existing solution base as away of transforming the business. For that reason, before we begin to explore the details of big data technology, we must probe the depths of the business drivers and market conditions that make big data a viable alternative within the enterprise.

1.2 UNDERSTANDING THE BUSINESS DRIVERS

The story begins at the intersection of the need for agility and the demand for actionable insight as the proportion of signal to noise decreases. Decreasing "time to market" for decision-making enhancements to all types of business processes has become a critical competitive differentiator. However, the user demand for insight that is driven by ever-increasing data volumes must be understood in the context of organizational business drivers to help your organization appropriately adopt a coherent information strategy as a prelude to deploying big data technology.

Corporate business drivers may vary by industry as well as by company, but reviewing some existing trends for data creation, use, sharing, and the demand for analysis may reveal how evolving market conditions bring us to a point where adoption of big data can become a reality.

Business drivers are about agility in utilization and analysis of collections of datasets and streams to create value: increase revenues, decrease costs, improve the customer experience, reduce risks, and increase productivity. The data explosion bumps up against the requirement for capturing, managing, and analyzing information. Some key trends that drive the need for big data platforms include the following:

- **Increased data volumes being captured and stored**: According to the 2011 IDC Digital Universe Study, "In 2011, the amount of information created and replicated will surpass 1.8 zettabytes, ... growing by a factor of 9 in just five years."[3] The scale of this growth surpasses the reasonable capacity of traditional relational database management systems, or even typical hardware configurations supporting file-based data access.

- **Rapid acceleration of data growth**: Just 1 year later, the 2012 IDC Digital Universe study ("The Digital Universe in 2020") postulated, "From 2005 to 2020, the digital universe will grow by a factor of 300, from 130 exabytes to 40,000 exabytes, or 40 trillion gigabytes (more than 5,200 gigabytes for every man, woman, and child in 2020). From now until 2020, the digital universe will about double every two years."[4]
- **Increased data volumes pushed into the network**: According to Cisco's annual Visual Networking Index Forecast, by 2016, annual global IP traffic is forecast to be 1.3 zettabytes.[5] This increase in network traffic is attributed to the increasing number of smartphones, tablets and other Internet-ready devices, the growing community of Internet users, the increased Internet bandwidth and speed offered by telecommunications carriers, and the proliferation of Wi-Fi availability and connectivity. More data being funneled into wider communication channels create pressure for capturing and managing that data in a timely and coherent manner.
- **Growing variation in types of data assets for analysis**: As opposed to the more traditional methods for capturing and organizing *structured* datasets, data scientists seek to take advantage of unstructured data accessed or acquired from a wide variety of sources. Some of these sources may reflect minimal elements of structure (such as Web activity logs or call detail records), while others are completely unstructured or even limited to specific formats (such as social media data that merges text, images, audio, and video content). To extract usable signal out of this noise, enterprises must enhance their existing structured data management approaches to accommodate semantic text and content-stream analytics.
- **Alternate and unsynchronized methods for facilitating data delivery**: In a structured environment, there are clear delineations of the

---

[3]2011 IDC Digital Universe Study: extracting value from chaos, <http://www.emc.com/collateral/demos/microsites/emc-digital-universe-2011/index.htm>.
[4]The Digital Universe in 2020, <http://www.emc.com/collateral/analyst-reports/idc-the-digital-universe-in-2020.pdf>.
[5]See Cisco Press Release of May 30, 2012, <http://newsroom.cisco.com/press-release-content?type=webcontent&articleId=888280>.

discrete tasks for data acquisition or exchange, such as bulk file transfers via tape and disk storage systems, or via file transfer protocol over the Internet. Today, data publication and exchange is full of unpredictable peaks and valleys, with data coming from a broad spectrum of connected sources such as websites, transaction processing systems, and even "open data" feeds and streams from government sources and social media networks like Twitter. This creates new pressures for rapid acquisition, absorption, and analysis while retaining currency and consistency across the different datasets.

- **Rising demand for real-time integration of analytical results**: There are more people—with an expanding variety of roles—who are consumers of analytical results. The growth is especially noticeable in companies where end-to-end business processes are augmented to fully integrate analytical models to optimize performance. As an example, a retail company can monitor real-time sales of tens of thousands of Stock Keeping Units (SKUs) at hundreds of retail locations, and log minute-by-minute sales trends. Delivering these massive datasets to a community of different business users for simultaneous analyses gives new insight and capabilities that never existed in the past: it allows buyers to review purchasing patterns to make more precise decisions regarding product catalog, product specialists to consider alternate means of bundling items together, inventory professionals to allocate shelf space more efficiently at the warehouse, pricing experts to instantaneously adjust prices at different retail locations directly at the shelf, among other uses. The most effective uses of intelligence demand that analytical systems must process, analyze, and deliver results within a defined time window.

1.3 LOWERING THE BARRIER TO ENTRY

Enabling business process owners to take advantage of analytics in many new and innovative ways has always appeared to be out of reach for most companies. And the expanding universe of created information has seemed to tantalizingly dangle broad-scale analytics capabilities beyond the reach of those but the largest corporations.

Interestingly, for the most part, much of the technology classified as "big data" is not new. Rather, it is the ability to package these techniques in ways that are accessible to organizations in ways that up until recently had been limited by budget, resource, and skills constraints, which are typical of smaller businesses. What makes the big data concept so engaging is that emerging technologies enable a broad-scale analytics capability with a relatively low barrier to entry.

As we will see, facets of technology for business intelligence and analytics have evolved to a point at which a wide spectrum of businesses can deploy capabilities that in the past were limited to the largest firms with equally large budgets. Consider the four aspects in Table 1.1.

The changes in the environment make big data analytics attractive to all types of organizations, while the market conditions make it practical. The combination of simplified models for development, commoditization, a wider palette of data management tools, and low-cost utility computing has effectively lowered the barrier to entry, enabling a much wider swath of organizations to develop and test out

Table 1.1 Contrasting Approaches in Adopting High-Performance Capabilities		
Aspect	**Typical Scenario**	**Big Data**
Application development	Applications that take advantage of massive parallelism developed by specialized developers skilled in high-performance computing, performance optimization, and code tuning	A simplified application execution model encompassing a distributed file system, application programming model, distributed database, and program scheduling is packaged within Hadoop, an open source framework for reliable, scalable, distributed, and parallel computing
Platform	Uses high-cost massively parallel processing (MPP) computers, utilizing high-bandwidth networks, and massive I/O devices	Innovative methods of creating scalable and yet elastic virtualized platforms take advantage of clusters of commodity hardware components (either cycle harvesting from local resources or through cloud-based utility computing services) coupled with open source tools and technology
Data management	Limited to file-based or relational database management systems (RDBMS) using standard row-oriented data layouts	Alternate models for data management (often referred to as NoSQL or "Not Only SQL") provide a variety of methods for managing information to best suit specific business process needs, such as in-memory data management (for rapid access), columnar layouts to speed query response, and graph databases (for social network analytics)
Resources	Requires large capital investment in purchasing high-end hardware to be installed and managed in-house	The ability to deploy systems like Hadoop on virtualized platforms allows small and medium businesses to utilize cloud-based environments that, from both a cost accounting and a practical perspective, are much friendlier to the bottom line

high-performance applications that can accommodate massive data volumes and broad variety in structure and content.

1.4 CONSIDERATIONS

While the market conditions suggest that there is a lowered barrier to entry for implementing big data solutions, it does not mean that implementing these technologies and business processes is a completely straightforward task. There is a steep learning curve for developing big data applications, especially when going the open source route, which demands an investment in time and resources to ensure the big data analytics and computing platform are ready for production. And while it is easy to test-drive some of these technologies as part of an "evaluation," one might think carefully about some key questions before investing a significant amount of resources and effort in scaling that learning curve, such as:

- **Feasibility**: Is the enterprise aligned in a way that allows for new and emerging technologies to be brought into the organization, tested out, and vetted without overbearing bureaucracy? If not, what steps can be taken to create an environment that is suited to the introduction and assessment of innovative technologies?
- **Reasonability**: When evaluating the feasibility of adopting big data technologies, have you considered whether your organization faces business challenges whose resource requirements exceed the capability of the existing or planned environment? If not currently, do you anticipate that the environment will change in the near-, medium- or long-term to be more data-centric and require augmentation of the resources necessary for analysis and reporting?
- **Value**: Is there an expectation that the resulting quantifiable value that can be enabled as a result of big data warrants the resource and effort investment in development and productionalization of the technology? How would you define clear measures of value and methods for measurement?
- **Integrability**: Are there any constraints or impediments within the organization from a technical, social, or political (i.e., policy-oriented) perspective that would prevent the big data technologies from being fully integrated as part of the operational architecture? What steps need to be taken to evaluate the means by which big data can be integrated as part of the enterprise?

- **Sustainability**: While the barrier to entry may be low, the costs associated with maintenance, configuration, skills maintenance, and adjustments to the level of agility in development may not be sustainable within the organization. How would you plan to fund continued management and maintenance of a big data environment?

In Chapter 2, we will begin to scope out the criteria for answering these questions as we explore the types of business problems that are suited to a big data solution.

1.5 THOUGHT EXERCISES

Here are some questions and exercises to ponder before jumping head-first into a big data project:

- What are the sizes of the largest collections of data to be subjected to capture, storage, and analysis within the organization?
- Detail the five most challenging analytical problems facing your organization. How would any of these challenges be addressed if the volume of data is increased by a factor of 10 and 100, respectively?
- Provide your own definition of what big data means to your organization.
- Develop a justification for big data within your organization in one sentence.
- Develop a single graphic image depicting what you believe to be the impact of increased data volumes and variety.
- Identify three "big data" sources, either within or external to your organization that would be relevant to your business.

CHAPTER 2

Business Problems Suited to Big Data Analytics

In Chapter 1, we identified some key market drivers for assessing how big data technologies might prove to be beneficial to an organization, including:

- the accelerating growth of data volumes to be consumed;
- the desire to blend both structured and unstructured data;
- lowered barrier to entry for enabling scalable high-performance analytics;
- reducing operational costs by leveraging commodity hardware;
- simplified programming and execution model for scalable applications.

In the past, the ability to acquire and deploy high-performance computing systems was limited to large organizations willing to teeter on the bleeding edge of technology. However, the convergence of the aforementioned market conditions has enhanced the attraction of high-performance computing to many different types of organizations now willing to invest in the effort of designing and implementing big data analytics. This is especially true for those organizations whose budgets were previously too puny to accommodate the investment.

2.1 VALIDATING (AGAINST) THE HYPE: ORGANIZATIONAL FITNESS

Even as the excitement around big data analytics reaches a fevered pitch, it remains a technology-driven activity. And as we speculated in Chapter 1, there are a number of factors that need to be considered before making a decision regarding adopting that technology. But all of those factors need to be taken into consideration; just because big data is feasible within the organization, it does not necessarily mean that it is *reasonable*.

Unless there are clear processes for determining the value proposition, there is a risk that it will remain a fad until it hits the disappointment phase of the hype cycle. At that point, hopes may be dashed when it becomes clear that the basis for the investments in the technology was not grounded in expectations for clear business improvements.

As a way to properly ground any initiatives around big data, one initial task would be to evaluate the organization's fitness as a combination of the five factors presented in Chapter 1: feasibility, reasonability, value, integrability, and sustainability. Table 2.1 provides a sample framework for determining a score for each of these factors ranging from 0 (lowest level) to 4 (highest level).

The resulting scores can be reviewed (an example of a radar chart is shown in Figure 2.1). Each of these variables is, for the most part, somewhat subjective, but there are ways of introducing a degree of objectivity, especially when considering the value of big data.

2.2 THE PROMOTION OF THE VALUE OF BIG DATA

That being said, a thoughtful approach must differentiate between hype and reality, and one way to do this is to review the difference between what is being *said* about big data and what is being *done* with big data. A scan of existing content on the "value of big data" sheds interesting light on what is being promoted as the expected result of big data analytics and, more interestingly, how familiar those expectations sound. A good example is provided within an economic study on the value of big data (titled "Data Equity—Unlocking the Value of Big Data"), undertaken and published by the Center for Economics and Business Research (CEBR) that speaks to the cumulative value of:

- optimized consumer spending as a result of improved targeted customer marketing;
- improvements to research and analytics within the manufacturing sectors to lead to new product development;
- improvements in strategizing and business planning leading to innovation and new start-up companies;
- predictive analytics for improving supply chain management to optimize stock management, replenishment, and forecasting;
- improving the scope and accuracy of fraud detection.[1]

[1]Center for Economics and Business Research Ltd. Data equity—unlocking the value of big data, April 2012. Downloaded from <http://www.sas.com/offices/europe/uk/downloads/data-equity-cebr. pdf> (Last accessed 08-08-13).

Table 2.1 Quantifying Organizational Readiness					
Score by Dimension	0	1	2	3	4
Feasibility	Evaluation of new technology is not officially sanctioned	Organization tests new technologies in reaction to market pressure	Organization evaluates and tests new technologies after market evidence of successful use	Organization is open to evaluation of new technology Adoption of technology on an *ad hoc* basis based on convincing business justifications	Organization encourages evaluation and testing of new technology Clear decision process for adoption or rejection Organization supports allocation of time to innovation
Reasonability	Organization's resource requirements for near-, mid-, and long-terms are satisfactorily met	Organization's resource requirements for near- and mid-terms are satisfactorily met, unclear as to whether long-term needs are met	Organization's resource requirements for near-term is satisfactorily met, unclear as to whether mid- and long-term needs are met	Business challenges are expected to have resource requirements in the mid- and long-terms that will exceed the capability of the existing and planned environment	Business challenges have resource requirements that clearly exceed the capability of the existing and planned environment Organization's go-forward business model is highly information-centric
Value	Investment in hardware resources, software tools, skills training, and ongoing management and maintenance exceeds the expected quantifiable value	The expected quantifiable value widely is evenly balanced by an investment in hardware resources, software tools, skills training, and ongoing management and maintenance	Selected instances of perceived value may suggest a positive return on investment	Expectations for some quantifiable value for investing in limited aspects of the technology	The expected quantifiable value widely exceeds the investment in hardware resources, software tools, skills training, and ongoing management and maintenance
Integrability	Significant impediments to incorporating any nontraditional technology into environment	Willingness to invest effort in determining ways to integrate technology, with some successes	New technologies can be integrated into the environment within limitations and with some level of effort	Clear processes exist for migrating or integrating new technologies, but require dedicated resources and level of effort	No constraints or impediments to fully integrate technology into operational environment

(Continued)

Table 2.1 (Continued)					
Score by Dimension	0	1	2	3	4
Sustainability	No plan in place for acquiring funding for ongoing management and maintenance costs No plan for managing skills inventory	Continued funding for maintenance and engagement is given on an *ad hoc* basis Sustainability is at risk on a continuous basis	Need for year-by-year business justifications for continued funding	Business justifications ensure continued funding and investments in skills	Program management office effective in absorbing and amortizing management and maintenance costs Program for continuous skills enhancement and training

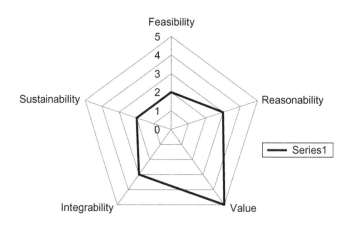

Figure 2.1 Radar chart example of readiness scores.

Curiously, these are exactly the same types of benefits promoted by business intelligence and data warehouse tools vendors and system integrators for the past 15−20 years, namely:

- Better targeted customer marketing
- Improved product analytics
- Improved business planning
- Improved supply chain management
- Improved analysis for fraud, waste, and abuse

Further articles, papers, and vendor messaging on big data reinforce these presumptions, but if these were the same improvements promised by wave after wave of new technologies, what makes big data different?

2.3 BIG DATA USE CASES

The answer must lie in the "democratization" of high-performance capabilities, which is inherent in the characteristics of the big data analytics application development environment. This environment largely consists of a methodology for elastically harnessing parallel computing resources and distributed storage, scalable performance management, along with data exchange via high-speed networks.

The result is improved performance and scalability, and we can examine another data point that provides self-reported descriptions using big data techniques, namely, the enumeration of projects listed at The Apache Software Foundation's PoweredBy Hadoop Web site (http://wiki.apache.org/hadoop/PoweredBy).

A scan of the list allows us to group most of those applications into these categories:

- **Business intelligence, querying, reporting, searching**, including many implementation of searching, filtering, indexing, speeding up aggregation for reporting and for report generation, trend analysis, search optimization, and general information retrieval.
- **Improved performance for common data management operations**, with the majority focusing on log storage, data storage and archiving, followed by sorting, running joins, extraction/transformation/loading (ETL) processing, other types of data conversions, as well as duplicate analysis and elimination.
- **Non-database applications**, such as image processing, text processing in preparation for publishing, genome sequencing, protein sequencing and structure prediction, web crawling, and monitoring workflow processes.
- **Data mining and analytical applications**, including social network analysis, facial recognition, profile matching, other types of text analytics, web mining, machine learning, information extraction, personalization and recommendation analysis, ad optimization, and behavior analysis.

In turn, the core capabilities that are implemented using the big data application can be further abstracted into more fundamental categories:

- **Counting** functions applied to large bodies of data that can be segmented and distributed among a pool of computing and storage resources, such as document indexing, concept filtering, and aggregation (counts and sums).
- **Scanning** functions that can be broken up into parallel threads, such as sorting, data transformations, semantic text analysis, pattern recognition, and searching.
- **Modeling** capabilities for analysis and prediction.
- **Storing** large datasets while providing relatively rapid access.

Generally, **Processing** applications can combine these core capabilities in different ways.

2.4 CHARACTERISTICS OF BIG DATA APPLICATIONS

What is interesting to note is that most of the applications reported by Hadoop users are not necessarily *new* applications. Rather, there are many familiar applications, except that the availability of a low-cost high-performance computing framework either allows more users to develop these applications, run larger deployments, or speed up the execution time. This, coupled with a further review of the different types of applications, suggests that of the limited scenarios discussed as big data success stories, the big data approach is mostly suited to addressing or solving business problems that are subject to one or more of the following criteria:

1. **Data throttling**: The business challenge has an existing solutions, but on traditional hardware, the performance of a solution is throttled as a result of data accessibility, data latency, data availability, or limits on bandwidth in relation to the size of inputs.
2. **Computation-restricted throttling**: There are existing algorithms, but they are heuristic and have not been implemented because the expected computational performance has not been met with conventional systems.
3. **Large data volumes**: The analytical application combines a multitude of existing large datasets and data streams with high rates of data creation and delivery.

4. **Significant data variety**: The + +data in the different sources vary in structure and content, and some (or much) of the data is unstructured.
5. **Benefits from data parallelization**: Because of the reduced data dependencies, the application's runtime can be improved through task or thread-level parallelization applied to independent data segments.

So what, how does this relate to business problems whose solutions are suited to big data analytics applications? These criteria can be used to assess the degree to which business problems are suited to big data technology. As a prime example, ETL processing is hampered by data throttling and computation throttling, can involve large data volumes, may consume a variety of different types of datasets, and can benefit from data parallelization. This is the equivalent of a big data "home run" application!

More examples are given in Table 2.2.

2.5 PERCEPTION AND QUANTIFICATION OF VALUE

So far we have looked at two facets of the appropriateness of big data, with the first being organizational fitness and the second being suitability of the business challenge. The third facet must also be folded into the equation, and that is big data's contribution to the organization. In essence, these facets drill down into the question of value and whether using big data significantly contributes to adding value to the organization by:

- Increasing revenues: As an example, an expectation of using a recommendation engine would be to increase same-customer sales by adding more items into the market basket.
- Lowering costs: As an example, using a big data platform built on commodity hardware for ETL would reduce or eliminate the need for more specialized servers used for data staging, thereby reducing the storage footprint and reducing operating costs.
- Increasing productivity: Increasing the speed for the pattern analysis and matching done for fraud analysis helps to identify more instances of suspicious behavior faster, allowing for actions to be taken more quickly and transform the organization from being focused on recovery of funds to proactive prevention of fraud.

Table 2.2 Examples of Applications Suited to Big Data Analytics		
Application	Characteristic	Sample Data Sources
Energy network monitoring and optimization	Data throttling	Sensor data from smart meters and network components
	Computation throttling	
	Large data volumes	
Credit fraud detection	Data throttling	Point-of-sale data
	Computation throttling	Customer profiles
	Large data volumes	Transaction histories
	Parallelization	Predictive models
	Data variety	
Data profiling	Large data volumes Parallelization	Sources selected for downstream repurposing
Clustering and customer segmentation	Data throttling	Customer profiles
	Computation throttling	Transaction histories
	Large data volumes	Enhancement datasets
	Parallelization	
	Data variety	
Recommendation engines	Data throttling	Customer profiles
	Computation throttling	Transaction histories
	Large data volumes	Enhancement datasets
	Parallelization	Social network data
	Data variety	
Price modeling	Data throttling	Point-of-sale data
	Computation throttling	Customer profiles
	Large data volumes	Transaction histories
	Parallelization	Predictive models

- Reducing risk: Using a big data platform or collecting many thousands of streams of automated sensor data can provide full visibility into the current state of a power grid, in which unusual events could be rapidly investigated to determine if a risk of an imminent outage can be reduced.

2.6 FORWARD THINKING ABOUT VALUE

While we continue employing big data technologies for developing algorithms and solutions that are new implementations of old algorithms, we must anticipate that there are, or will be, opportunities for new solution paradigms using parallel execution and data distribution in innovative ways. Yet without proper organizational preparedness, neither approach is likely to succeed. In Chapter 3, we will discuss different aspects of corporate readiness in preparation for designing, developing, and implementing big data applications.

2.7 THOUGHT EXERCISES

Given the premise of considering the suitability of your business challenges, here are some questions and exercises to ponder:

- Using the organizational fitness criteria described in this chapter, assess the degree to which your organization is suited to evaluating big data.
- List what you believe to be the three business challenges in your organization that are most suitable candidates for big data.
- For each of those business challenges, list the characteristics that make it suited to big data.
- Who are the people in your organization with experience, knowledge, or training in big data? How well do they understand your business problem?

CHAPTER 3

Achieving Organizational Alignment for Big Data Analytics

The seemingly ubiquitous use of the term "big data" somewhat simplifies the technical landscape in ways that hide a level of complexity that can confuse potential organizational stakeholders. Big data is not a single out-of-the-box product. In fact, there are numerous aspects of big data techniques and technologies, each with its own technical appeal: hardware analytical appliances, software tools that employ commodity hardware, NoSQL and graph-based data management systems, analytics tools, as well as the many components and programming frameworks encompassed within Apache's open-source Hadoop project.

As we suggested in Chapter 1, market conditions coupled with lowered barriers to entry have enabled individuals within an organization to "test-drive" a combination of big data techniques. Yet before any of these new technologies can be fully incorporated within production business processes, they must win adoption in a broader enterprise setting in ways that add measurable value.

3.1 TWO KEY QUESTIONS

Given this need, managers need to answer two essential questions:

1. **Demonstration of value**: What is the process for piloting technologies to determine their feasibility and business value and for engaging business sponsors and socializing the benefits of a selected technique?
2. **Operationalization**: What must happen to bring big data analytics into organization's system development life cycle to enable their use?

Answering both of these questions is key to differentiating between adoption of new technologies for their own sake as opposed to improving business processes by virtue of transformative methods supported by selected new technologies.

The first question is intended to channel the energy and effort of test-driving big data technologies in the context of one or more real business problems to determine whether those technologies add value. But more importantly, presuming that the technology is valuable, the goal of the first question is to devise a communication strategy for sharing the message to the right people within the organization to identify a champion, secure business sponsorship, and establish bidirectional engagement to keep the business sponsors educated and aware of progress.

The second question is where the rubber meets the road. Once a decision is made to adopt big data, the goal of this question is to develop the tactics for the information technologists to work with the data management professionals and the business stakeholders to migrate the big data projects into the production environment in a controlled and managed way without disrupting day-to-day operations.

3.2 THE HISTORICAL PERSPECTIVE TO REPORTING AND ANALYTICS

These questions become much more relevant when you realize that the expectations for usability of big data clash with existing approaches for business intelligence (BI), reporting and analytics, as well as the end-to-end data integration, data collection, and consolidation and aggregation in the traditional data warehouse (DW) model.

That warrants some perspective on the history of that traditional model. The data warehouse model itself has undergone a series of refinements in reaction to a continuous need for increased performance and shortened cycles for delivering actionable knowledge. The business driver for the data warehouse largely focused on providing reports from transactional systems without interfering with the operational performance of those systems. Transaction processing data models and systems are engineered to accommodate updates to a few records at a time, and the transaction processing application systems are optimized to enable short response time to facilitate user productivity.

Alternatively, the expectation for decision support and reporting processes was to be able to review aggregations of many records at the same time. That meant that decision support processing must enable access of large amounts of data from multiple operational systems. These system expectations are mutually exclusive: optimizing for either can severely impact the performance of the other.

Preserving optimal response time for transaction processing systems meant a downgrading of the priority of reporting and analysis tasks. The result was the model of the data warehouse—a segregated system intended to support querying and reporting of collected, consolidated, and aggregated data in a way that did not impact the performance of the transaction processing systems.

The conventional strategy is information fragmentation and reorganization. Datasets are extracted from the source systems and loaded into online analytical processing (OLAP) systems or other analytical appliances and tuned to meet the anticipated performance needs for analytical queries. At the same time, datasets are replicated according to geography to finesse data latency and avoid network bottlenecks. Yet this fragmented information topology has unnecessarily complicated the information architecture and artificially impedes the ability to provide real-time reporting and analytics.

Subsequently, much of our effort is spent accommodating the decision to fragment data. That fact is a key motivating factor in setting expectations for big data.

3.3 THE CULTURE CLASH CHALLENGE

On the one hand, enterprises have invested much time and resources in developing an architecture for querying, reporting, and analysis that allows for dimensional analysis: "slicing and dicing" the data along different dimensions such as geography, business function, IT function, variant data domains (e.g., "customer" vs "product"), or time.

On the other hand, though, users, especially of the data scientist variety, are increasingly dissatisfied with the dimensional shackles that have become the foundation of the data warehouse. As an example, one recurring concern of data scientists performing fraud analysis is that the information technology practitioners who have organized the data in a data warehouse to support rapid report generation and fast query responses may have filtered out potentially interesting bits of information.

So while data warehouses are good for streaming data into spreadsheets, they are limited when it comes to undirected data discovery—creating demand from analysts for "access to the raw data" in a big data environment instead of funneling requests through a business intelligence team assigned to query the data warehouse.

3.4 CONSIDERING ASPECTS OF ADOPTING BIG DATA TECHNOLOGY

This dynamic reveals a tension between the traditional data warehouse approach and the rising demand for new analytical tools that enable more and different queries from more users than before. Within that dynamic, organizations need to find a way to evaluate whether the new technologies are valuable and how they can be incorporated into the information management structure and effectively deployed. The complexity of the challenge becomes more apparent once you consider some aspects of adoption of the big data techniques:

- **Steep learning curve**: While some of the technology is basically "plug and play," much involves a steep learning curve. It is easy to download open-source software for Hadoop/MapReduce, a tuple-based data environment, or a graph-based database system. But it is much harder to develop applications that use these platforms unless the developer has some experience in data distribution and high performance/parallel code development.
- **Data life cycle changes**: The data life cycle demands for big data analytics differ from data systems supporting traditional transaction processing as well as data warehouses and data marts that typically deliver results based on static structured datasets. A prime example is the desire to stream live data directly into a big data analytical application for real-time integration, while data warehouses are often just populated with static datasets extracted from existing front-end systems.
- **Existing infrastructure**: A decade (or more) of investment in the traditional data warehouse/business intelligence framework has institutionalized certain approaches to data management, yet the decision about the existing infrastructure (such as the traditional approaches to extracting data from sources to load into the warehouse as opposed to newer approaches to federation and virtualization that allow the data to remain in its original source) impacts access to

synchronized datasets as well as usability of a variety of data sources that are expected to feed big data analytics.

- **Existing investment**: The phrase referenced in the previous bullet bears repeating. Organizations have sunk significant investments in developing a BI/DW environment, and some consideration must be applied to assess the degree to which one wants to either salvage or abandon that investment.
- **Data intent**: Most data instances are created for specific purposes, but big data applications seek to repurpose data for analysis. The original data intent may differ drastically from an array of potential uses, and this implies the need for greater governance for data control, quality, and semantic consistency.
- **Size and duration**: The desire to acquire and use massive datasets has direct implications for the "pure" aspects of data management. The transitory characteristics associated with rapid turnaround of numerous data streams conflicts with the desire to retain very large datasets in anticipation of the potential for new analyses to be performed in the future. This tension will force enterprises to make investment and capital acquisition decisions to support data persistence and retention.

3.5 INVOLVING THE RIGHT DECISION MAKERS

Given these challenges, how can organizations plan to support big data? More to the point: Who in the organization needs to be involved in the process of acquiring, proving, and then deploying big data solutions, and what are their roles and responsibilities?

In any technology adoption cycle, it is incumbent upon the key stakeholders in the organization to make sure that the business process owners, the information consumers, the technical infrastructure innovators, the application developers, and the enterprise architects all work together in an environment that can continue to satisfy existing reporting needs yet is flexible enough for exploratory work.

We can look at a general sequence of tasks (Figure 2.1) to help us consider how to manage the transition into a production development process to take advantage of the business value big data techniques can provide. The sequence starts with recognizing this opportunity, then defining expectations, and piloting, vetting, and assessing big data technology before moving into production.

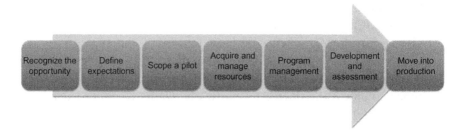

Figure 3.1 The process of validating big data and moving it into production.

1. **Recognize the opportunity**: Use the criteria in Chapter 2 to identify the business challenges that have the most to gain from adopting one or more of the big data techniques.
2. **Define expectations**: Articulate specific value improvement expectations within a bounded time frame. These expectations are the basis for a later go/no-go decision.
3. **Scope a pilot**: Spec out the framework for what concepts are to be proven during the development and evaluation of a pilot application.
4. **Acquire and manage resources**: Identify and acquire the skills necessary for big data development.
5. **Program management**: Devise a program plan for the pilot phase as well as anticipate the tasks for migration into production.
6. **Development and assessment**: Design, develop, code, test, and evaluate whether the result meets expectations.
7. **Move into production**: If the technology appears to add value, strengthen the plan to move it into production.

3.6 ROLES OF ORGANIZATIONAL ALIGNMENT

Executing this sequence in alignment with organizational needs requires people who can champion new technologies while also retaining a critical eye to differentiate between hype and reality. Aside from the boots-on-the ground folks like big data developers and data scientists, below are some roles of organizational alignment played during the consideration, evaluation, and decisioning process for assessing the value proposition for big data:

• **Business evangelist**: This individual understands the types of performance barriers imposed by the existing technical infrastructure and understands that ongoing reviews of emerging technology may create efficiencies that do not currently exist within the organization. The job of the business evangelist is to socialize the value of exploring the use of new techniques among the business process owners and to solicit their input to understand their current and future needs to guide the selection of technologies to review and possibly pilot.

- **Technical evangelist**: The technical evangelist understands the emerging technology and the science behind new methods, where the technology can potentially improve the application environment, either by improving the performance of existing processes or by enabling new capabilities.
- **Business analyst**: This is the person who engages the business process owners and solicits their needs and expectations. This process identifies some of the key quantifiable measures for evaluating the business benefits of the new technology, as well as frames the technical requirements for any pilot project.
- **Big data application architect**: While the vendor community suggests that these new programming frameworks simplify the process of developing applications for big data platforms, any solution that is designed without a firm background in parallel and distributed computing is bound to be sensitive to fundamental flaws that will impede the optimal performance. Make sure that any pilot development is designed by an application architect with reasonable experience in performance computing.
- **Application developer**: Identify the technical resources with the right set of skills for programming and testing parallel and distributed applications.
- **Program manager**: Lastly, and perhaps most importantly, engage a program manager with project management expertise to plan and oversee any pilot development to make sure that it remains aligned with organizational expectations, remains within an allocated budget, and is properly documented to ensure that the best practices can be captured and migrated into production.

The evangelist roles are critical in establishing recognition of the value proposition, and the business and technical evangelists must work with the program manager and the architects in mapping out a strategy for engaging the business users, understanding how the new techniques can deliver greater value in a more efficient or rapid manner, as well as agree to the success measures and criteria for the inevitable go/no-go decision. The business analysts must communicate their visibility into the business challenges to the application developers, and both must be governed by the program manager to reduce the risk of wasted investment in technology development purely for technology's sake.

Having a well-planned and managed program for technology evaluation in the context of well-defined business needs will simplify organizational alignment: it casts all speculative technical development in the context of demonstrating (or not) the creation of business value. Soliciting clear business requirements and specifying corroborating success criteria and measures enables a level of trust that test-driving new technology like big data analytics is not purely an intellectual exercise, but rather is a repeatable process for injecting new ideas into the corporation.

3.7 THOUGHT EXERCISES

Given the premise of achieving organizational alignment, here are some questions and exercises to ponder:

- For each of your organization's business functions, identify one or two potential business champions/evangelists for big data.
- Using what you have learned through discussions with key stakeholders, come up with three elevator pitch sentences describing the expectation for value for big data in fifteen seconds or less.
- Have you adequately identified the skill sets necessary for evaluating big data technology? List the key skills and capabilities and identify individuals within the organization who currently have some experience with those skills.
- If there is a skills gap, what are your three key sources for climbing the learning curve?
- Provide an argument for ripping out the entire data warehouse infrastructure and replacing it with big data.
- Provide an argument for dovetailing big data as just one component of the existing business intelligence, reporting, and analytics infrastructure.

Developing a Strategy for Integrating Big Data Analytics into the Enterprise

As with any innovative technology that promises business value, many individuals have rushed to embrace big data and big data analytics as a supplementary source, if not the primary source of reporting and analytics for the enterprise. And as with the adoption of any new technology, it is important to realize that even with lowered barriers to entry, there are still going to be challenges and issues that become apparent when new technologies are rapidly brought into the organization with the expectation that they will be quickly mainstreamed into production.

Clearly, it would be unwise to commit to a new technology without assessing its potential value for improving existing processes or creating new opportunities. This value is manifested in terms of increased profitability, reduced organizational risk, or enhanced customer experience (among others) in relation to the costs associated with the technology's introduction and continued maintenance and operations. Essentially, testing and piloting technology is necessary to maintain an enterprise's competitiveness and ensure the new technology is feasible for implementation. This can only be done when there are measures for success and acceptability that are clearly defined in the context of these dimensions of business value.

But in many organizations, the processes to expeditiously mainstream new techniques and tools often bypass business value justification, existing program governance, or corporate best practices designed to ensure new technologies work with existing systems. Pilot projects are initiated just to check out the new technology, without any guidance from the business. The result is that pilot projects that are prematurely moved into "production" are really just point solutions relying on islands of data that neither scale from the performance perspective nor fit into the enterprise from an architectural perspective.

4.1 DECIDING WHAT, HOW, AND WHEN BIG DATA TECHNOLOGIES ARE RIGHT FOR YOU

The adoption of big data technology is reminiscent of other technology adoption cycles in the past. Some examples include the acquisition of customer relationship management (CRM) systems or the desire to use XML for an extremely broad spectrum of data-oriented activities. The issue is that even if these are disruptive methods that have the potential to increase value, the paths by which the techniques and algorithms insinuate themselves are often in ways that might not be completely aligned with the corporate strategy or the corporate culture. This may be because the organization is not equipped to make best use of the technology.

Yet enterprises need to allow experimentation to test-drive new technologies in ways that conform to proper program management and due diligence. For example, implementing a CRM system will not benefit the company until users of the system are satisfied with the quality of the customer data and are properly trained to make best use of customer data to improve customer service and increase sales. In other words, the implementation of the technology must be coupled with a strategy to employ that technology for business benefit.

4.2 THE STRATEGIC PLAN FOR TECHNOLOGY ADOPTION

A strategic plan for adopting big data technologies within the reporting, analytics, and business intelligence environment is meant to achieve balance between the need for agility in adopting innovative analytics methods and continued operations within the existing environment. The strategic plan should guide the evolution of data management architectures in ways that are aligned with corporate vision and governance. That strategy will incorporate aspects of exploration for the viability and feasibility of new techniques. This should result in selecting those techniques that best benefit the organization, as well as provide support for moving those techniques into the production environment.

The strategy would at the very least incorporate these key points:

- ensuring that there are standard processes for soliciting input from the business users;

- Specifying clear evaluation criteria for acceptability and adoption;
- Providing guidance for preparing the data environment for massive data scalability;
- Promoting the concept of data reuse;
- Instituting oversight and governance for the innovation activity;
- Streamlining the methods for mainstreaming accepted technologies.

4.3 STANDARDIZE PRACTICES FOR SOLICITING BUSINESS USER EXPECTATIONS

Frequently, the enthusiasm of the IT department for a new technology overwhelms the processes for establishing grounded business justifications for evaluating and eventually adopting it. Project plans focus on the delivery of the capability in ways that demonstrate that progression is made toward a technical implementation yet neglect solving specific business problems. In turn, as components of the technology are delivered and milestones are reached, there is a realization that the product does not address the end-user expectations. This realization triggers a redesign (in the best case) or abandonment (in the worst case).

Whether the big data activity is driven by the business users or the technologists, it is critical to engage the business users early on in the process to understand the types of business challenges they face so that you can gauge their expectations and establish their success criteria. Clearly defining the performance expectation for big data reporting and analytics means linking business value to business utilization of the technology.

Engage the business users by asking them what they want to achieve using the new techniques, how those expectations support the company's overall corporate vision, how the execution is aligned with the strategic business objectives, and how to align technical milestones with business deliverables. Directly interact with the business function leaders as partners. Enlist their active participation as part of the requirements gathering stage, and welcome their input and suggestions during the design, testing, and implementation.

As part of the strategic plan, develop a standard template for business user engagement that minimally includes:

- Interview questions that can be used to understand the business opportunities.

- A value matrix in which potential areas of improvement attributable to big data are documented (Table 4.1). Use this to initially document the business expectations, as a prelude to the next phase in which the success criteria are defined.
- Business calendar that can be used to align technical progression with business imperatives.

4.4 ACCEPTABILITY FOR ADOPTION: CLARIFY GO/NO-GO CRITERIA

Allocating time, resources, and budget on testing out new technologies is a valid use of research & development spending. However, at some point, a decision must be made to either embrace the technology that is being tested and move it into production, or to recognize that it may not meet the business's needs, and move along to the next opportunity.

Before embarking on any design and development activity, collaborate with the business users utilizing their specific corporate value metrics to provide at least five quantitative performance measures that will reflect the success of the technology. State a specific expected improvement associated with a dimension of value, assert a minimal but measurable level of acceptable performance that must be achieved, and provide an explicit time frame within which the level of acceptable performance is to be reached. This method will solidify the success criteria, which benefits both the business users and the technologists. This benefits the business user by providing clear guidelines for acceptability. For the technologists, the benefit provided is an audit trail that demonstrates that the technology has business value and is not perceived to simply be the pursuit of an intellectual exercise.

For example, if the big data application is intended to monitor customer sentiment, an example performance measure might be "decrease customer call center issue resolution time by 15% within 3 weeks after

Table 4.1 An Example Value Matrix			
Value Dimension One of (Revenue, Expenses, Productivity, Risk, Customer Experience)	Report/ Analysis	Measure	Expected Improvement

an acute issue is identified." Another example might be "increase cross-sell volume by 20% as a result of improved recommendations within 10 days after each analysis." These discrete quantitative measures can be used to make that go/no-go decision as to whether to move forward or to pull the plug.

Failing to establish a structure around this process can lead to issues. In many cases, making this decision on incomplete metrics or irrelevant measures may lead to one of several potential unfounded outcomes:

- committing to the methods even when it may not make sense;
- killing a project before it has been determined to add value, or worse;
- deferring the decision, effectively continuing to commit resources without having an actionable game plan for moving the technology into production.

4.5 PREPARE THE DATA ENVIRONMENT FOR MASSIVE SCALABILITY

Big data volumes may threaten to overwhelm an organization's existing infrastructure for data acquisition for analytics, especially if the technical architecture is organized around a traditional data warehouse information flow. Test-driving big data techniques can be done in a virtual sandbox environment, which can be iteratively configured and reconfigured to suit the needs of the technology. However, the expectation that any big data tools and technologies would be mainstreamed also implies a need for applying corresponding operations, maintenance, security, and business continuity standards that are relevant for any system.

The sandbox approach itself must be reevaluated. Developing an application "in the small" that uses a small subset of the anticipated data volumes can mask performance issues that may be hard to overcome without forethought. Some straightforward examples include:

- **Staging**: Do you expect to move input data directly into a big data platform, or will there be a need for a staging area at which datasets are delivered and held until they are ready to load? If so, recognize that the data volumes may impose a need to scale up the staging capability, or alternatively you must incorporate a staging plan as part of the big data application itself.

- **Data streaming**: Where are the datasets sourced, and will they be provided on a streaming basis? If so, that means scaling up the networking and I/O capacities to support the eventual speeds and volumes.
- **Computation**: Many statistical analysis algorithms have computational requirements that are proportional to orders of magnitude of the data provided, and in exponential algorithms, the demand ramps up very quickly. A small sandbox may not exhibit the same computation demand as a larger environment, so understand the need for computational performance and how it needs to scale.

Applying a standard for scaling the environment means the enterprise needs to adjust its operations and systems maintenance model to presume the existence of massive data volumes. Considerations to address include using high-speed networks; enabling high-performance data integration tools such as data replication, change data capture, compression, and alternate data layouts to rapidly load and access data; and enabling large-scale backup systems.

4.6 PROMOTE DATA REUSE

Big data analytics holds the promise of creating value through the collection, integration, and analysis of many large, disparate datasets. Different analyses will employ a variety of data sources, implying the potential need to use the same datasets multiple times in different ways. Data reuse has specific ramifications to the environment and implies that the data management architecture must support capture and access to these datasets in a consistent and predictable manner.

That suggests some visibility into data use from an enterprise perspective. Enterprise architects must be engaged to review which datasets are replicated, which information sources can be adopted in different ways, and what the expectations must be for consistency, synchronization, speed of delivery, as well as archiving and retention as these sources of information are used in different ways.

To meet this need, the enterprise should possess capabilities that include increased data archiving and massive-scale standardization to ensure level of trust in the data. The enterprise should also be prepared to address other implications such as enforcing a level of precise data synchronizations across multiple sources or using data virtualization tools to smoothen both semantics and latency in data access. The organization's information and business intelligence strategy must detail plans for large-scale data management accessibility and quality as part of the enterprise information architecture.

4.7 INSTITUTE PROPER LEVELS OF OVERSIGHT AND GOVERNANCE

A recurring theme involves navigating the boundary between speculative application development, assessing pilot projects and when successful, and then transitioning those pilots into the mainstream. This cannot be done without some oversight and governance. Governance will properly direct the alignment of speculative development with achieving business goals in relation to the collected business requirements. Incorporating oversight of innovative activities within a well-defined strategic program plan helps hamper the evolution of "shadow IT" practices that bypass the standard approval processes.

A good example is the interest in cloud-based services such as hosted CRM. Many business people may try to deploy a CRM solution by signing up for cloud-based tools and populating these tools with data extracted from among the various corporate databases. However, data that is migrated to that hosted system can often no longer be monitored or controlled according to corporate data policies and guidelines. This allows a degradation in the usability of the data and affects synchronization and consistency of data and processes.

An alternate approach is to fully incorporate innovation projects within the corporate governance framework to provide the senior management with full visibility into, and awareness of the potential value of new technologies. This allows management to track the execution of proofs of concept, monitor the progress, and help determine the degree to which the technology is suited to solving specific business problems. At the same time, the governance policies can include the specification of those "go/no-go" success criteria as well as the methods for assessing those criteria prior to adopting the technology and incorporating it into the organizational technology architecture.

4.8 PROVIDE A GOVERNED PROCESS FOR MAINSTREAMING TECHNOLOGY

Any speculative development using new technology is vetted using the concept of a "pilot project" or a "proof of concept." But once the pilot is completed and the concept has been proven, then what? If the project demonstrates clear value based on the success criteria and a decision is made to adopt the technology, you must have a plan to move the system into a production design and development phase.

A technology adoption plan will specify the details for transitioning from an experimental phase to a production design phase. That will include:

- identifying the need for additional resources;
- assembling a development environment;
- assembling a testing environment;
- assessing the level of effort for design, development, and implementation;
- identifying staffing requirements;
- providing a program plan for running and managing the technology in the enterprise over time.

This process is essential for big data technologies. Big data has some particular needs, such as scalable computing platforms for developing high-performance algorithms, acquiring the computing as well as the increased storage to accommodate the massive volumes of data. It important to not neglect upgrading the information architecture to support the analysis of many massive datasets, including semantic metadata, "meaning-based" and "context-based" analysis, high-performance data integration, and scalable data quality management.

4.9 CONSIDERATIONS FOR ENTERPRISE INTEGRATION

Reflecting back on our sample performance and success measures, presume that a pilot big data recommendation analytics engine *did* demonstrate the targeted improvement for increased revenues, decreased costs, or any of the other specified success metrics. Meeting these objectives means that the proof of concept was successful. In turn, an objective evaluation would lead to the recommendation that the application be devised for migration into production via the approved system development lifecycle processes and channels for design, development, testing, and implementation.

This approach to developing a strategy for integrating big data analytics is one in which the business users are directly engaged in providing input to articulate the value proposition, gain alignment across business functions, and help prioritize activities. The approach means that any successful pilot project can be mainstreamed within an implementation plan that will guide the current development while reducing the complexity of enhancements and extensibility in future development. Doing so will not just reduce the complexity and pain that is often associated with "shoehorning" application code into the enterprise architecture.

Rather, taking these steps will help ensure that the design and development are fully integrated within the organization's project governance, information technology governance, and information governance frameworks. This will ensure consistency with business objectives while observing the IT governance protocols for moving applications into production. Using this approach helps to ensure that new applications can be more easily integrated within the existing business intelligence, reporting, and analytics infrastructure and provide maximum value to a broad constituency across the organization.

4.10 THOUGHT EXERCISES

Given the premise of strategic planning, here are some questions and exercises to ponder:

- Recall three experiences with evaluating and adopting new technologies. What were the most valuable lessons learned regarding the successful implementation?
- What lessons might be relevant to the implementation of a big data solution in your environment?
- What would you have done differently?
- Over time, did the new technologies deliver on the original promise?
- At which point during a technology evaluation did you engage the business users? Was that the right time? Why?

CHAPTER 5

Data Governance for Big Data Analytics: Considerations for Data Policies and Processes

It should not come as a surprise that in a big data environment, much like *any* environment, the end users might have concerns about the believability of analytical results. This is particularly true when there is limited visibility into trustworthiness of the data sources. One added challenge is that even if the producers of the data sources are known, the actual derivation of the acquired datasets may still remain opaque. Striving for data trustworthiness has driven the continued development and maturation of processes and tools for data quality assurance, data standardization, and data cleansing. In general, data quality is generally seen as a mature discipline, particularly when the focus is evaluating datasets and applying remedial or corrective actions to data to ensure that the datasets are fit for the purposes for which they were originally intended.

5.1 THE EVOLUTION OF DATA GOVERNANCE

In the past 5 years or so, there have been a number of realizations that have, to some extent, disrupted this perception of "data quality maturity," namely:

- **Correct versus correction**: In many environments, tools are used to *fix* data, not to ensure that the data is valid or correct. What was once considered to be the cutting edge in terms of identifying and then fixing data errors has, to some extent, fallen out of favor in lieu of process-oriented validation, root cause analysis, and remediation.
- **Data repurposing**: More organizational stakeholders recognize that datasets created for one functional purpose within the enterprise (such as sales, marketing, accounts payable, or procurement to name a few) are used multiple times in different contexts, particularly for reporting and analysis. The implication is that data quality can no longer be measured in terms of "fitness for purpose," but instead must be evaluated in terms of "fitness for *purposes*," taking all downstream uses and quality requirements into account.

- **The need for oversight**: This realization, which might be considered a follow-on to the first, is that ensuring the usability of data for all purposes requires more comprehensive oversight. Such oversight should include monitored controls incorporated into the system development life cycle and across the application infrastructure.

These realizations lead to the discipline called data governance. Data governance describes the processes for defining corporate data policies, describing processes for operationalizing observance of those policies, along with the organizational structures that include data governance councils and data stewards put in place to monitor, and hopefully ensure compliance with those data policies.

Stated simply, the objective of data governance is to institute the right levels of control to achieve one of three outcomes:

1. **Alert**: Identify data issues that might have negative business impact.
2. **Triage**: Prioritize those issues in relation to their corresponding business value drivers.
3. **Remediate**: Have data stewards take the proper actions when alerted to the existence of those issues.

When focused internally, data governance not only enables a degree of control for data created and shared within an organization, it empowers the data stewards to take corrective action, either through communication with the original data owners or by direct data intervention (i.e., "correcting bad data") when necessary.

5.2 BIG DATA AND DATA GOVERNANCE

Naturally, concomitant with the desire for measurably high quality information in a big data environment is the inclination to institute "big data governance." It is naive, however, to assert that when it comes to big data governance one should adopt the traditional approaches to data quality. Furthermore, one cannot assume that just because vendors, system integrators, and consultants stake their claims over big data by stressing the need for "big data quality" that the same methods and tools can be used to monitor, review, and correct data streaming into a big data platform.

Upon examination, the key characteristics of big data analytics are not universally adaptable to the conventional approaches to data quality and data governance. For example, in a traditional approach to data quality, levels of data usability are measured based on the idea of "data quality dimensions," such as:

- **Accuracy**, referring to the degree to which the data values are correct.
- **Completeness**, which specifies the data elements that must have values.
- **Consistency** of related data values across different data instances.
- **Currency**, which looks at the "freshness" of the data and whether the values are up to date or not.
- **Uniqueness**, which specifies that each real-world item is represented once and only once within the dataset.

These types of measures are generally intended to validate data using defined rules, catch any errors when the input does not conform to those rules, and correct recognized errors when the situations allow it. This approach typically targets moderately sized datasets, from known sources, with structured data, with a relatively small set of rules. Operational and analytical applications of limited size can integrate data quality controls, alerts, and corrections, and those corrections will reduce the downstream negative impacts.

5.3 THE DIFFERENCE WITH BIG DATASETS

On the other hand, big datasets neither exhibit these characteristics, nor do they have similar types of business impacts. Big data analytics is generally centered on consuming massive amounts of a combination of structured and unstructured data from both machine-generated and human sources. Much of the analysis is done without considering the business impacts of errors or inconsistencies across the different sources, from where the data originated, or how frequently it is acquired.

Big data applications look at many input streams originating from within and outside the organization, some taken from a variety of social networking streams, syndicated data streams, news feeds, preconfigured search filters, public or open-sourced datasets, sensor networks, or other unstructured data streams. Such diverse datasets resist singular approaches to governance.

When the acquired datasets and data streams originate outside the organization, there is little facility for control over the input. The original sources are often so obfuscated that there is little capacity to even know who created the data in the first place, let alone enable any type of oversight over data creation.

Another issue involves the development and execution model for big data applications. Data analysts are prone to develop their own models in their private sandbox environments. In these cases, the developers often bypass traditional IT and data management channels, opening greater possibilities for inconsistencies with sanctioned IT projects. This is complicated more as datasets are tapped into or downloaded directly without IT's intervention.

Consistency (or the lack thereof) is probably the most difficult issue. When datasets are created internally and a downstream user recognizes a potential error, that issue can be communicated to the originating system's owners. The owners then have the opportunity to find the root cause of the problems and then correct the processes that led to the errors.

But with big data systems that absorb massive volumes of data, some of which originates externally, there are limited opportunities to engage process owners to influence modifications or corrections to the source. On the other hand, if you opt to "correct" the recognized data error, you are introducing an inconsistency with the original source, which at worst can lead to incorrect conclusions and flawed decision making.

5.4 BIG DATA OVERSIGHT: FIVE KEY CONCEPTS

The conclusion is that the standard approach to data governance in which data policies defined by an internal governance council direct control of the usability of datasets cannot be universally applied to big data applications. And yet there is definitely a need for some type of oversight that can ensure that the datasets are usable and that the analytic results are trustworthy. One way to address the need for data quality and consistency is to leverage the concept of data policies based on the information quality characteristics that are important to the big data project.

This means considering the intended uses of the results of the analyses and how the inability to exercise any kind of control on the original sources of the information production flow can be mitigated by the users on the consumption side. This approach requires a number of key concepts for data practitioners and business process owners to keep in mind:

- managing consumer data expectations;
- identifying the critical data quality dimensions;
- monitoring consistency of metadata and reference data as a basis for entity extraction;
- repurposing and reinterpretation of data;
- data enrichment and enhancement when possible.

5.4.1 Managing Consumer Data Expectations

There may be a wide variety of users consuming the results of the spectrum of big data analytics applications. Many of these applications use an intersection of available datasets. Analytics applications are supposed to be designed to provide actionable knowledge to create or improve value. The quality of information must be directly related to the ways the business processes are either expected to be improved by better quality data or how ignoring data problems leads to undesired negative impacts, and there may be varied levels of interest in asserting levels of usability and acceptability for acquired datasets by different parties.

This means, for the scope of the different big data analytics projects, you must ascertain these collective user expectations by engaging the different consumers of big data analytics to discuss how quality aspects of the input data that might affect the computed results. Some examples include:

- datasets that are out of sync from a time perspective (e.g., one dataset refers to today's transactions being compared to pricing data from yesterday);
- not having all the datasets available that are necessary to execute the analysis;
- not knowing if the data element values that feed the algorithms taken from different datasets share the same precision (e.g., sales per minute vs sales per hour);

- not knowing if the values assigned to similarly named data attributes truly share the same underlying meaning (e.g., is a "customer" the person who pays for our products or the person who is entitled to customer support?).

Engaging the consumers for requirements is a process of discussions with the known end users, coupled with some degree of speculation and anticipation of who the pool of potential end users are, what they might want to do with a dataset, and correspondingly, what their levels of expectation are. Then, it is important to establish how those expectations can be measured and monitored, as well as the realistic remedial actions that can be taken.

5.4.2 Identifying the Critical Dimensions of Data Quality

An important step is to determine the dimensions of data quality that are relevant to the business and then distinguish those that are only measurable from those that are both measurable and controllable. This distinction is important, since you can use the measures to assess usability when you cannot exert control and to make corrections or updates when you do have control. In either case, here are some dimensions for measuring the quality of information used for big data analytics:

- **Temporal consistency**: Measuring the timing characteristics of datasets used in big data analytics to see whether they are aligned from a temporal perspective.
- **Timeliness**: Measuring if the data streams are delivered according to end-consumer expectations.
- **Currency**: Measuring whether the datasets are up to date.
- **Completeness**: Measuring that all the data is available.
- **Precision consistency**: Assessing if the units of measure associated with each data source share the same precision and if those units are properly harmonized if not.
- **Unique identifiability**: Focusing on the ability to uniquely identify entities within datasets and data streams and link those entities to known system of record information.
- **Semantic consistency**: This metadata activity may incorporate a glossary of business terms, hierarchies and taxonomies for business concepts, and relationships across concept taxonomies for standardizing ways that entities identified in structured and unstructured data are tagged in preparation for data use.

5.4.3 Consistency of Metadata and Reference Data for Entity Extraction

Big data analytics is often closely coupled with the concept of text analytics, which depends on contextual semantic analysis of streaming text and consequent entity concept identification and extraction. But before you can aspire to this kind of analysis, you need to ground your definitions within clear semantics for commonly used reference data and units of measure, as well as identifying aliases used to refer to the same or similar ideas.

Analyzing relationships and connectivity in text data is key to entity identification in unstructured text. But because of the variety of types of data that span both structured and unstructured sources, one must be aware of the degree to which unstructured text is replete with nuances, variation, and double meanings. There are many examples of this ambiguity, such as references to a *car*, a *minivan*, an *SUV*, a *truck*, a *roadster*, as well as the manufacturer's company name, make, or model—all referring to an automobile.

These concepts are embedded in the value within a context, and are manifested as metadata tags, keywords, and categories that are often recognized as the terms that drive how search engine optimization algorithms associate concepts with content. Entity identification and extraction depend on the differentiation between words and phrases that carry high levels of "meaning" (such as person name, business names, locations, or quantities) from those that are used to establish connections and relationships, mostly embedded within the language of the text.

As data volumes expand, there must be some process for definition (and therefore control) over concept variation in source data streams. Introducing conceptual domains and hierarchies can help with semantic consistency, especially when comparing data coming from multiple source data streams.

Be aware that context carries meaning; as there are different inferences about data concepts and relationship, you can make based on the identification of concept entities known within your reference data domains and how close they are found in the data source or stream. But since the same terms and phrases may have different meanings depending on the participating constituency generating the content, it yet again highlights the need for precision in semantics associated with concepts extracted from data sources and streams.

5.4.4 Repurposing and Reinterpretation

One of the foundational concepts for the use of data for analytics is the possibility of finding interesting patterns that can lead to actionable insight, and you must keep in mind that any acquired dataset may be used for any potential purpose at any time in the future. However, this strategy of data reuse can also backfire. Repeated copying and repurposing leads to a greater degree of separation between data producer and data consumer. With each successive reuse, the data consumers yet again must reinterpret what the data means. Eventually, any inherent semantics associated with the data when it is created evaporates.

Governance will also mean establishing some limits around the scheme for repurposing. New policies may be necessary when it comes to determining what data to acquire and what to ignore, which concepts to capture and which ones should be trashed, the volume of data to be retained and for how long, and other qualitative data management and custodianship policies.

5.4.5 Data Enrichment and Enhancement

It is hard to consider any need for data governance or quality for large acquired datasets without discussing alternatives for data cleansing and correction. The plain truth is that in general you will have no control over the quality and validity of data that is acquired from outside the organization. Validation rules can be used to score the usability of the data based on end-user requirements, but if those scores are below the level of acceptability and you still want to do the analysis, you basically have these choices:

1. Don't use the data at all.
2. Use the data in its "unacceptable" state and modulate your users' expectations in relation to the validity score.
3. Change the data to a more acceptable form.

This choice might not be as drastic as you might think. If the business application requires accuracy and precision in the data, attempting to use unacceptable data will introduce a risk that the results may not be trustworthy. On the other hand, if you are analyzing extremely large datasets for curious and interesting patterns or to identify relationships among many different entities, there is some leeway for executing the process in the presence of a small number of errors. A minimal percentage of data flaws will not significantly skew the results.

As an example, large online retailers want to drive increased sales through relationship analysis, as well as look at sales correlations within sales "market baskets" (the collection of items purchased by an individual at one time). When processing millions of (or orders of magnitude more) transactions a day, a minimal number of inconsistencies, incomplete records, or errors are likely to be irrelevant.

However, should incorrect values be an impediment to the analysis and making changes does not significantly alter the data from its original form other than in a positive and expected way, data enhancement and enrichment may be a reasonable alternative. A good example is address standardization. Address locations may be incomplete or even incorrect (e.g., the zip code may be incorrect). Standardizing an address's format and applying corrections is a consistent way only to improve the data.

The same could be said for linking extracted entities to known identity profiles using algorithms that match identities with high probability. Making that link enhances the analysis through the sharing of profile information for extracted entities. A similar process can be used in connection with our defined reference metadata hierarchies and taxonomies: standardizing references to items or concepts in relation to a taxonomic order lets your application treat *cars*, *automobiles*, *vans*, *minivans*, *SUVs*, *trucks*, and *RVs* as *vehicles*, at least for certain analytical purposes.

5.5 CONSIDERATIONS

Data governance is still somewhat in its infancy, and it is challenging to attempt to adapt a collection of organizational frameworks designed for a controllable environment to a big data world in which there are limits to the amount of control that can be exercised over the data. Defining "big data governance" policies around these practice areas (managing consumer data expectations, defining critical data quality dimensions, managing the consistency of metadata and reference data, allowing for data repurposing, and data enrichment and enhancement) can help you institute a level of trust in analytical results.

5.6 THOUGHT EXERCISES

Given the premise of data governance for big data, here are some questions and exercises to ponder:

- What are the three most critical dimensions of data quality your business data consumers care about for analytics? Why?
- How would you specify methods for measuring compliance with the consumers' expectations?
- What are some frequently used reference datasets (such as countries, states, currencies) that would be useful to standardize?
- Document the data flow for five acquired datasets from entry to the organization to presentation of analytical results. What is the average number of times each dataset is used?
- Look at five analytical applications and characterize the need for data correction and enhancement based on the need for accuracy and precision.

CHAPTER 6

Introduction to High-Performance Appliances for Big Data Management

Big data analytics applications combine the means for developing and implementing algorithms that must access, consume, and manage data. In essence, the framework relies on a technology ecosystem of components that must be combined in a variety of ways to address each application's requirements, which can range from general information technology (IT) performance scalability to detailed performance improvement objectives associated with specific algorithmic demands.

For example, some algorithms expect that massive amounts of data are immediately available quickly, necessitating large amounts of core memory. Other applications may need numerous iterative exchanges of data between different computing nodes, which would require high-speed networks.

The big data technology ecosystem stack may include:

- Scalable **storage** systems that are used for capturing, manipulating, and analyzing massive datasets.
- A **computing platform**, sometimes configured specifically for large-scale analytics, often composed of multiple (typically multicore) processing nodes connected via a high-speed network to memory and disk storage subsystems. These are often referred to as **appliances**.
- A **data management** environment, whose configurations may range from a traditional database management system scaled to massive parallelism to databases configured with alternative distributions and layouts, to newer graph-based or other NoSQL data management schemes.
- An **application development framework** to simplify the process of developing, executing, testing, and debugging new application code. This framework should include programming models, development tools, program execution and scheduling, and system configuration and management capabilities.

- Layering packaged methods of scalable **analytics** (including statistical and data mining models) that can be configured by the analysts and other business consumers to help improve the ability to design and build analytical and predictive models.
- Oversight and **management** processes and tools that are necessary to ensure alignment with the enterprise analytics infrastructure and collaboration among the developers, analysts, and other business users.

In this chapter, we examine the storage, appliance, and data management aspects of this ecosystem.

6.1 USE CASES

To motivate the discussion, it is worth looking at four typical big data analytics use cases chosen from among the characteristics implementations discussed in Chapter 2:

1. Targeted customer marketing, in which customer profiles are analyzed for the purpose of formulating customized marketing campaigns to influence customer purchase behaviors.
2. Social media analytics applications that scan through streams of social media channels looking for positive or negative sentiments that are correlated to the behavior of a collective of individuals.
3. Fraud detection algorithms that analyze historical patterns of activity looking for suspicious behaviors that are indicative of fraud or abuse, as well as scanning transactions in real time looking for aberrant behavior requiring further investigation.
4. Web site recommendation engines that lever large sets of historical transaction patterns combined with customer profiles to identify suggested additional items to be presented to the customer as potential add-on purchases.

Table 6.1 provides some considerations for storage, appliance hardware, and data management related to the use case.

6.2 STORAGE CONSIDERATIONS: INFRASTRUCTURE BEDROCK FOR THE DATA LIFECYCLE

In any environment intended to support the analysis of massive amounts of data, there must be the infrastructure supporting the data lifecycle from acquisition, preparation, integration, and execution. The

Table 6.1 Considerations for Some Examples of Big Data Applications			
Analytics Use Case	Storage Considerations	Appliance Considerations	Data Management Considerations
Improving targeted customer marketing	Must combine streamed data for analysis with customer profiles typically stored in a data warehouse.	Hardware appliances that can support traditional data warehouse models as well as analytical environments may be preferred.	Customer profiles are likely to be managed using a standard data warehouse using dimensional models. Analytic algorithms may require more flexible data structures such as hash tables or graph.
Social media analytics	Depending on the amount of information to be streamed, may require a large storage footprint with high-speed I/O to handle the volume. However, since the data stream quickly and value instantiation may be transient, this application may be tolerant of failures.	Much of the discussions around the use of scalable high-performance analytic engines centers on social media analytics, with Hadoop deployed across various hardware configurations a popular choice.	These applications have a high reliance on algorithmic execution, but may also require entity extraction and identity resolution, necessitating a combination of traditional data management and NoSQL platforms.
Fraud detection	Depending on the application there will be a need for capturing and managing large amounts of data over long periods of time.	Depends on the size of the analysis. Larger environments will require scalable and elastic computational platforms.	Fraud detection combines continuous analysis in search of patterns that can be related to individuals or cohorts that may either be known or unknown. This suggests a need for a variety of different analytical models that can be integrated with traditional relational data models.
Web site recommendations engine	For large eCommerce applications, the amount of data is proportional to both the number of visitors and the average number of web events per visitor, potentially resulting in massive amounts of data requiring a large, scalable storage footprint. As with social media analytics, there may be some tolerance to failures.	The determination of hardware versus software appliances is related to the performance expectations. The need for real time or immediate computations and responses may dictate the need for dedicated hardware systems.	As with other big data applications, this will need to combine static profile information with dynamic calculations associated with real-time activity, requiring a combination of traditional data warehouse and more eclectic models that can be deployed using NoSQL style frameworks.

need to acquire and manage massive amounts of data suggests a need for specialty storage systems to accommodate the big data applications. When evaluating specialty storage offerings, some variables to consider include:

- **Scalability**, which looks at whether expectations for performance improvement are aligned with the additional of storage resources, and the degree to which the storage subsystem can support massive data volumes of increasing size.
- **Extensibility**, which examines how flexible the storage system's architecture is in allowing the system to be grown without the constraint of artificial limits.
- **Accessibility**, which looks at any limitations or constraints in providing simultaneous access to an expanding user community without compromising performance.
- **Fault tolerance**, which imbues the storage environment with the capability to recover from intermittent failures.
- **High-speed I/O capacity**, which measures whether the input/output channels can satisfy the demanding timing requirements for absorbing, storing, and sharing large data volumes.
- **Integratability**, which measures how well the storage environment can be integrated into the production environment.

Often, the storage framework involves a software layer for managing a collection of storage resources and providing much of these capabilities. The software configures storage for replication to provide a level of fault tolerance, as well as managing communications using standard protocols (such as UDP or TCP/IP) among the different processing nodes. In addition, some frameworks will replicate stored data, providing redundancy in the event of a fault or failure.

6.3 BIG DATA APPLIANCES: HARDWARE AND SOFTWARE TUNED FOR ANALYTICS

Because big data applications and analytics demand a high level of system performance that exceeds the capabilities of typical systems, there is a general need for using scalable multiprocessor configurations tuned to meet mixed-used demand for reporting, ad hoc analysis, and more complex analytical models. And as can be seen in relation to the example use cases in Table 6.1, there are going to be a plethora of performance drivers for computational scalability, with respect to data volumes and the number of simultaneous users. Naturally, the technical leaders must assess the end-users' scalability requirements to help in selecting a specific architectural approach.

There are essentially two approaches to configuring a high-performance architecture platform. One (the hardware appliance approach) employs specialty-hardware configurations, while the other (the software appliance approach) uses software to manage a collection of commodity hardware components.

Hardware appliances are often configured as multiprocessor systems, although the architectures may vary in relation to the ways that different memory components are configured. There are different facets of the system that contribute to maximizing system performance, including CPU/core configurations, cache memory, core memory, flash memory, temporary disk storage areas, and persistent disk storage. Hardware architects consider the varying configurations of these levels of the memory hierarchy to find the right combination of memory devices with varying sizes, costs, and speed to achieve the right level of performance and scalability and provide optimal results by satisfying the ability to respond to increasingly complex queries, while enabling simultaneous analyses.

Different architectural configurations address different scalability and performance issues in different ways, so when it comes to deciding which type of architecture is best for your analytics needs, consider different alternatives including symmetric multiprocessor (SMP) systems, massively parallel processing (MPP), as well as software appliances that adapt to parallel hardware system models.

Hardware appliances are designed for big data applications. They often will incorporate multiple (multicore) processing nodes and multiple storage nodes linked via a high-speed interconnect. Support tools are usually included as well to manage high-speed integration connectivity and enable mixed configurations of computing and storage nodes.

A **software appliance** for big data is essentially a suite of high-performance software components that can be layered on commodity hardware. Software appliances can incorporate database management software coupled with a high-performance execution engine and query optimization to support and take advantage of parallelization and data distribution. Vendors may round out the offering by providing application development tools, analytics capabilities, as well as enable direct user tuning with alternate data layouts for improved performance.

6.4 ARCHITECTURAL CHOICES

Analytical environments are deployed in different architectural models. Even on parallel platforms, many databases are built on a **shared-everything** approach in which the persistent storage and memory components are all shared by the different processing units. A **shared-disk** approach may have isolated processors, each with its own memory, but the persistent storage on disk is still shared across the system. These types of architectures are layered on top of SMP machines. While there may be applications that are suited to this approach, there are bottlenecks that exist because of the sharing, because all I/O and memory requests are transferred (and satisfied) over the same bus. As more processors are added, the synchronization and communication needs increase exponentially, and therefore the bus is less able to handle the increased need for bandwidth. This means that unless the need for bandwidth is satisfied, there will be limits to the degree of scalability.

In contrast, in a **shared-nothing** approach, each processor has its own dedicated disk storage. This approach, which maps nicely to an MPP architecture, is not only more suitable to discrete allocation and distribution of the data, it enables more effective parallelization, and consequently does not introduce the same kind of bus bottlenecks from which the SMP/shared-memory and shared-disk approaches suffer.

6.5 CONSIDERING PERFORMANCE CHARACTERISTICS

When it comes to big data, both the software and the hardware approaches are appealing to the nascent large-scale data analysts. However, there may be contrary perceptions of the benefits of selecting one of these approaches over the other, and Table 6.2 looks at how each supports some of the desired characteristics listed earlier in this book.

Table 6.2 Comparing Software and Hardware Approaches		
Characteristic	Software Based	Hardware Based
Data volumes	• Can handle petabytes (or possibly scale up to greater orders of magnitude)	• Can handle terabytes and can scale to petabytes
Performance and scalability	• With automatic parallelization you can achieve linear scaling, even with greater numbers of nodes • Communication is potential performance bottleneck • When application is not collocated with the data, channels for data loading may be a potential bottleneck • Incrementally adding nodes is easy	• Designed for rapid access for analytic purposes (queries, reports, OLAP) • Shared-nothing approach provides eminent scalability • Direct operation on compressed columnar data improves performance • Compression decreases amount of data to be paged in and out of memory, and consequently, disk I/O
Data integration	• Supports structured, unstructured, and streaming data • Potentially high communication cost for internode data exchange	• Supports structured data • Supports real-time analytics • Less amenable to integration with unstructured data
Fault tolerance	• Software models can be designed to withstand worker failure without restarting a process • Software approach may allow for larger clusters of 50–4000 nodes	• Generally assume infrequent failures and rely on underlying fault-tolerance techniques (e.g., RAID or replication). • Small and medium size (8–64 nodes) clusters are less likely to experience failures than clusters with hundreds of thousands of nodes
Heterogeneity	• Can potentially (but not typically) be deployed across a heterogeneous cluster • Can be deployed in a cloud	• Can potentially (but not typically) be deployed across a heterogeneous cluster • Performance may suffer when deployed on heterogeneous cluster • Can be deployed in a cloud
Knowledge delivery	• Is a programming model • Requires external repository for comparisons with previous analyses • Executes in batch • Not intended for interactive access	• Provides interactive access (ad hoc queries) • Provides interface to business intelligence front ends • Feeds analytic tools • Supports comparisons and trends

6.6 ROW- VERSUS COLUMN-ORIENTED DATA LAYOUTS AND APPLICATION PERFORMANCE

Awareness of the different latency costs associated with the different levels of the memory hierarchy inform the different ways that data can be stored and shared, especially because the alignment and orientation of data on disk can significantly impact the performance of analytical applications. Most traditional database systems employ a row-oriented layout, in which all the values associated with a specific row are laid out consecutively in memory. That layout may work well for transaction processing applications that focus on updating specific records associated with a limited number of transactions (or transaction steps) at a time.

On the other hand, big data analytics applications scan, aggregate, and summarize over massive datasets. These are manifested as algorithmic scans of are performed using multiway joins; accessing whole rows at a time when only the values of a smaller set of columns are needed may flood the network with extraneous data that is not immediately needed and ultimately will increase the execution time.

In other words, analytical applications and queries will only need to access the data elements needed to satisfy join conditions. With row-oriented layouts, the entire record must be read in order to access the required attributes, with significantly more data read than is needed to satisfy the request. Also, the row-oriented layout is often misaligned with the characteristics of the different types of memory systems (core, cache, disk, etc.), leading to increased access latencies. Subsequently, row-oriented data layouts will not enable the types of joins or aggregations typical of analytic queries to execute with the anticipated level of performance (Figure 6.1).

That is why a number of software appliances for big data use a database management system that uses an alternate, columnar layout for data that can help to reduce the negative performance impacts of data latency that plague databases with a row-oriented data layout. The values for each column can be stored separately, and because of this, for any query, the system is able to selectively access the specific

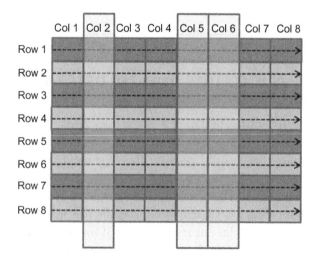

Figure 6.1 In a row-oriented database, accessing specific columns requires reading all records.

column values requested to evaluate the join conditions. Instead of requiring separate indexes to tune queries, the data values themselves within each column form the index. This speeds up data access while reducing the overall database footprint, while dramatically improving query performance (Figure 6.2).

The simplicity of the columnar approach provides many benefits, especially for those seeking a high-performance environment to meet the growing needs of extremely large analytic datasets, as can be seen by the example facets of performance discussed in Table 6.3.

6.7 CONSIDERING PLATFORM ALTERNATIVES

When considering the different ways of deploying an analytics environment, the key decisions for investing in infrastructure focus on how the platform best meets the expected performance needs. One must be willing to specify key measures for system performance to properly assess scalability requirements for the intended analytical applications to help select a specific architectural approach.

The benefits of using hardware appliances for big data center on engineering and integration. They are engineered for high-performance reporting and analytics, yet have a flexible architecture allowing integrated components to be configured to meet specific application needs.

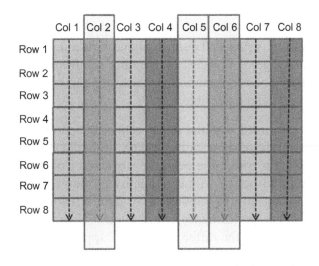

Figure 6.2 In a column-oriented database, only the columns in the query need to be retrieved.

Table 6.3 Comparing Row and Column Orientation for Data Management Layouts		
	Row Oriented	**Column Oriented**
Access performance	Limited in supporting many simultaneous diverse queries.	Engineered to enable selective traversal of the required columns aligned along commonly used caching strategies, which increases data access speed.
Speed of joins and aggregation	The need to stream entire records into memory to find the join attributes severely hampers performance by adding significant average access latency.	Data access streaming along column-oriented data allows for rapid join condition evaluation as well as incrementally computing the results of aggregate functions. Multiple processing units accessing and aggregating different columns in parallel increases overall query performance.
Suitability to compression	Difficult to apply compression in any way that increases performance.	The columnar alignment exposes opportunities for compressing data that can result in a significant decrease in storage needs while maintaining high performance. When employing an enumeration approach, there is no associated decompression burden, thereby not incurring additional computational load.
Data load speed	In a row-based arrangement, all of the data values in each row need to be stored together, and the inherent dependencies prevent parallel loading.	The columnar layout allows one to segregate data element storage by column, which means that each column could, in principle, be stored separately. This would allow the database system to load columns in parallel using multiple threads.

And while there is a capital investment in machinery, hardware appliances are low cost when compared to massive data warehouse hardware systems.

One benefit of using software appliances, meanwhile, is that they can take advantage of low-cost commodity hardware components. In addition, the reliance on commodity hardware allows a software appliance to be elastic and extensible.

However, you must consider all aspects of the performance needs of the different types of applications: data scalability, user scalability, access and loading speed, the need for workload isolation, reliance on parallelization and optimization, reliability in the presence of failures, the dependence on storage duplication or data distribution and replication, among other performance expectations. Then examine how the performance needs of the different types of applications are addressed by each of the architectures. This will provide a measurable methodology for assessing technology suitability.

6.8 THOUGHT EXERCISES

Given the premise of approaches to appliance architectures, here are some questions and exercises to ponder:

- For the three most typical big data application types, describe your expectations for data storage needs, what type of appliance is best, and what are the data management needs?
- Develop a scoring scale between 1 and 5 (where 1 represents a low need and 5 represents a great need) for each of the variables considered for storage requirements (extensibility, accessibility, fault tolerance, I/O speed, integratability). Rate your three applications using your defined scale.
- What are the variables you would consider for assessing the comparable costs and benefits of a software appliance versus a hardware appliance?

CHAPTER 7

Big Data Tools and Techniques

7.1 UNDERSTANDING BIG DATA STORAGE

As we have discussed in much of the book so far, most, if not all big data applications achieve their performance and scalability through deployment on a collection of storage and computing resources bound together within a runtime environment. In essence, the ability to design, develop, and implement a big data application is directly dependent on an awareness of the architecture of the underlying computing platform, both from a hardware and more importantly from a software perspective.

One commonality among the different appliances and frameworks is the adaptation of tools to leverage the combination of collections of four key computing resources:

1. **Processing capability**, often referred to as a CPU, processor, or node. Generally speaking, modern processing nodes often incorporate multiple *cores* that are individual CPUs that share the node's memory and are managed and scheduled together, allowing multiple tasks to be run simultaneously; this is known as *multithreading*.
2. **Memory**, which holds the data that the processing node is currently working on. Most single node machines have a limit to the amount of memory.
3. **Storage**, providing persistence of data—the place where datasets are loaded, and from which the data is loaded into memory to be processed.
4. **Network**, which provides the "pipes" through which datasets are exchanged between different processing and storage nodes.

Because single-node computers are limited in their capacity, they cannot easily accommodate massive amounts of data. That is why the high-performance platforms are composed of collections of computers in which the massive amounts of data and requirements for processing can be distributed among a pool of resources.

7.2 A GENERAL OVERVIEW OF HIGH-PERFORMANCE ARCHITECTURE

Most high-performance platforms are created by connecting multiple nodes together via a variety of network topologies. Specialty appliances may differ in the specifics of the configurations, as do software appliances. However, the general architecture distinguishes the management of computing resources (and corresponding allocation of tasks) and the management of the data across the network of storage nodes, as is seen in Figure 7.1.

In this configuration, a master job manager oversees the pool of processing nodes, assigns tasks, and monitors the activity. At the same time, a storage manager oversees the data storage pool and distributes datasets across the collection of storage resources. While there is no *a priori* requirement that there be any colocation of data and processing tasks, it is beneficial from a performance perspective to ensure that the threads process data that is local, or close to minimize the costs of data access latency.

To get a better understanding of the layering and interactions within a big data platform, we will examine the Apache Hadoop software stack, since the architecture is published and open for review. Hadoop is essentially a collection of open source projects that are

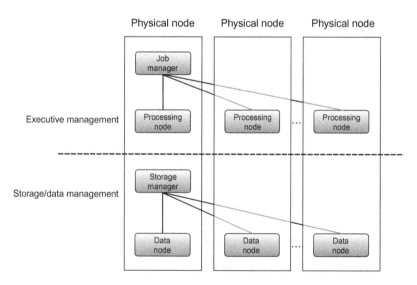

Figure 7.1 Typical organization of resources in a big data platform.

combined to enable a software-based big data appliance. We begin with the core aspects of Hadoop's utilities, upon which the next layer in the stack is propped, namely Hadoop distributed file systems (HDFS) and MapReduce. A new generation framework for job scheduling and cluster management is being developed under the name YARN.

7.3 HDFS

HDFS attempts to enable the storage of large files, and does this by distributing the data among a pool of data nodes. A single name node (sometimes referred to as NameNode) runs in a cluster, associated with one or more data nodes, and provide the management of a typical hierarchical file organization and namespace. The name node effectively coordinates the interaction with the distributed data nodes. The creation of a file in HDFS appears to be a single file, even though it blocks "chunks" of the file into pieces that are stored on individual data nodes.

The name node maintains metadata about each file as well as the history of changes to file metadata. That metadata includes an enumeration of the managed files, properties of the files, and the file system, as well as the mapping of blocks to files at the data nodes. The data node itself does not manage any information about the logical HDFS file; rather, it treats each data block as a separate file and shares the critical information with the name node.

Once a file is created, as data is written to the file, it is actually cached in a temporary file. When the amount of the data in that temporary file is enough to fill a block in an HDFS file, the name node is alerted to transition that temporary file into a block that is committed to a permanent data node, which is also then incorporated into the file management scheme.

HDFS provides a level of fault tolerance through data replication. An application can specify the degree of replication (i.e., the number of copies made) when a file is created. The name node also manages replication, attempting to optimize the marshaling and communication of replicated data in relation to the cluster's configuration and corresponding efficient use of network bandwidth. This is increasingly important in larger environments consisting of multiple racks of data servers, since communication among nodes on the same rack is generally faster than between server node sin different racks. HDFS attempts to maintain awareness of data node locations across the hierarchical configuration.

In essence, HDFS provides performance through distribution of data and fault tolerance through replication. The result is a level of robustness for reliable massive file storage. Enabling this level of reliability should be facilitated through a number of key tasks for failure management, some of which are already deployed within HDFS while others are not currently implemented:

- **Monitoring**: There is a continuous "heartbeat" communication between the data nodes to the name node. If a data node's heartbeat is not heard by the name node, the data node is considered to have failed and is no longer available. In this case, a replica is employed to replace the failed node, and a change is made to the replication scheme.
- **Rebalancing**: This is a process of automatically migrating blocks of data from one data node to another when there is free space, when there is an increased demand for the data and moving it may improve performance (such as moving from a traditional disk drive to a solid-state drive that is much faster or can accommodate increased numbers of simultaneous accesses), or an increased need to replication in reaction to more frequent node failures.
- **Managing integrity**: HDFS uses checksums, which are effectively "digital signatures" associated with the actual data stored in a file (often calculated as a numerical function of the values within the bits of the files) that can be used to verify that the data stored corresponds to the data shared or received. When the checksum calculated for a retrieved block does not equal the stored checksum of that block, it is considered an integrity error. In that case, the requested block will need to be retrieved from a replica instead.
- **Metadata replication**: The metadata files are also subject to failure, and HDFS can be configured to maintain replicas of the corresponding metadata files to protect against corruption.
- **Snapshots**: This is incremental copying of data to establish a point in time to which the system can be rolled back.[1]

---

[1]Some very good information is available in Hanson J. An introduction to the Hadoop distributed file system, accessed via <http://www.ibm.com/developerworks/library/wa-introhdfs> Another good resource is Apache's HDFS Architecture Guide, accessed via <http://hadoop.apache.org/docs/stable/hdfs_design.html>.

These concepts map to specific internal protocols and services that HDFS uses to enable a large-scale data management file system that can run on commodity hardware components. The ability to use HDFS solely as a means for creating a scalable and expandable file system for maintaining rapid access to large datasets provides a reasonable value proposition from an Information Technology perspective:

- decreasing the cost of specialty large-scale storage systems;
- providing the ability to rely on commodity components;
- enabling the ability to deploy using cloud-based services;
- reducing system management costs.

7.4 MAPREDUCE AND YARN

While MapReduce is discussed in greater detail in Chapter 8, it is valuable to both introduce the general concept of job control and management. In Hadoop, MapReduce originally combined both job management and oversight and the programming model for execution. The MapReduce execution environment employs a master/slave execution model, in which one master node (called the JobTracker) manages a pool of slave computing resources (called TaskTrackers) that are called upon to do the actual work.

The role of the JobTracker is to manage the resources with some specific responsibilities, including managing the TaskTrackers, continually monitoring their accessibility and availability, and the different aspects of job management that include scheduling tasks, tracking the progress of assigned tasks, reacting to identified failures, and ensuring fault tolerance of the execution. The role of the TaskTracker is much simpler: wait for a task assignment, initiate and execute the requested task, and provide status back to the JobTracker on a periodic basis. Different clients can make requests from the JobTracker, which becomes the sole arbitrator for allocation of resources.

There are limitations within this existing MapReduce model. First, the programming paradigm is nicely suited to applications where there is locality between the processing and the data, but applications that demand data movement will rapidly become bogged down by network latency issues. Second, not all applications are easily mapped to the MapReduce model, yet applications developed using alternative programming methods would still need the MapReduce system for job management. Third, the allocation of processing nodes within the cluster is fixed through allocation of certain nodes as "map slots" versus "reduce slots." When the computation is weighted toward one of the phases, the nodes assigned to the other phase are largely unused, resulting in processor underutilization.

This is being addressed in future versions of Hadoop through the segregation of duties within a revision called YARN. In this approach, overall resource management has been centralized while management of resources at each node is now performed by a local NodeManager. In addition, there is the concept of an ApplicationMaster that is associated with each application that directly negotiates with the central ResourceManager for resources while taking over the responsibility for monitoring progress and tracking status. Pushing this responsibility to the application environment allows greater flexibility in the assignment of resources as well as be more effective in scheduling to improve node utilization.

Last, the YARN approach allows applications to be better aware of the data allocation across the topology of the resources within a cluster. This awareness allows for improved colocation of compute and data resources, reducing data motion, and consequently, reducing delays associated with data access latencies. The result should be increased scalability and performance.[2]

7.5 EXPANDING THE BIG DATA APPLICATION ECOSYSTEM

At this point, a few key points regarding the development of big data applications should be clarified. First, despite the simplicity of downloading and installing the core components of a big data development and execution environment like Hadoop, designing, developing, and deploying analytic applications still requires some skill and expertise. Second, one must differentiate between the tasks associated with application design and development and the tasks associated with architecting the big data system, selecting and connecting its components, system configuration, as well as system monitoring and continued maintenance.

---

[2]An excellent description can be found in a series beginning with Murthy A. Introducing Apache Hadoop YARN, accessed via <http://hortonworks.com/blog/introducing-apache-hadoop-yarn/>.

In other words, transitioning from an experimental "laboratory" system into a production environment demands more than just access to the computing, memory, storage, and network resources. There is a need to expand the ecosystem to incorporate a variety of additional capabilities, such as configuration management, data organization, application development, and optimization, as well as additional capabilities to support analytical processing. Our examination of a prototypical big data platform engineered using Hadoop continues by looking at a number of additional components that might typically be considered as part of the ecosystem.

7.6 ZOOKEEPER

Whenever there are multiple tasks and jobs running within a single distributed environment, there is a need for configuration management and synchronization of various aspects of naming and coordination. The project's web page specifies it more clearly: "Zookeeper is a centralized service for maintaining configuration information, naming, providing distributed synchronization, and providing group services."[3]

Zookeeper manages a naming registry and effectively implements a system for managing the various static and ephemeral named objects in a hierarchical manner, much like a file system. In addition, it enables coordination for exercising control over shared resources that are impacted by race conditions (in which the expected output of a process is impacted by variations in timing) and deadlock (in which multiple tasks vying for control of the same resource effectively lock each other out of any task's ability to use the resource). Shared coordination services like those provided in Zookeeper allow developers to employ these controls without having to develop them from scratch.

7.7 HBASE

HBase is another example of a nonrelational data management environment that distributes massive datasets over the underlying Hadoop framework. HBase is derived from Google's BigTable and is a column-oriented data layout that, when layered on top of Hadoop, provides a fault-tolerant method for storing and manipulating large

---

[3]See <http://zookeeper.apache.org/>.

data tables. As was discussed in Chapter 6, data stored in a columnar layout is amenable to compression, which increases the amount of data that can be represented while decreasing the actual storage footprint. In addition, HBase supports in-memory execution.

HBase is not a relational database, and it does not support SQL queries. There are some basic operations for HBase: **Get** (which access a specific row in the table), **Put** (which stores or updates a row in the table), **Scan** (which iterates over a collection of rows in the table), and **Delete** (which removes a row from the table). Because it can be used to organize datasets, coupled with the performance provided by the aspects of the columnar orientation, HBase is a reasonable alternative as a persistent storage paradigm when running MapReduce applications.

7.8 HIVE

One of the often-noted issues with MapReduce is that although it provides a methodology for developing and executing applications that use massive amounts of data, it is not more than that. And while the data can be managed within files using HDFS, many business applications expect representations of data in structured database tables. That was the motivation for the development of Hive, which (according to the Apache Hive web site[4]) is a "data warehouse system for Hadoop that facilitates easy data summarization, ad-hoc queries, and the analysis of large datasets stored in Hadoop compatible file systems." Hive is specifically engineered for data warehouse querying and reporting and is not intended for use as within transaction processing systems that require real-time query execution or transaction semantics for consistency at the row level.

Hive is layered on top of the file system and execution framework for Hadoop and enables applications and users to organize data in a structured data warehouse and therefore query the data using a query language called HiveQL that is similar to SQL (the standard Structured Query Language used for most modern relational database management systems). The Hive system provides tools for extracting/transforming/loading data (ETL) into a variety of different data formats. And because the data warehouse system is built on top of

[4]See <http://hive.apache.org/>.

Hadoop, it enables native access to the MapReduce model, allowing programmers to develop custom Map and Reduce functions that can be directly integrated into HiveQL queries. Hive provides scalability and extensibility for batch-style queries for reporting over large datasets that are typically being expanded while relying on the fault-tolerant aspects of the underlying Hadoop execution model.

7.9 PIG

Even though the MapReduce programming model is relatively straightforward, it still takes some skill and understanding of both parallel and distributed programming and Java to best take advantage of the model. The Pig project is an attempt at simplifying the application development process by abstracting some of the details away through a higher level programming language called Pig Latin. According to the project's web site[5], Pig's high-level programming language allows the developer to specify how the analysis is performed. In turn, a compiler transforms the Pig Latin specification into MapReduce programs.

The intent is to embed a significant set of parallel operators and functions contained within a control sequence of directives to be applied to datasets in a way that is somewhat similar to the way SQL statements are applied to traditional structured databases. Some examples include generating datasets, filtering out subsets, joins, splitting datasets, removing duplicates. For simple applications, using Pig provides significant ease of development, and more complex tasks can be engineered as sequences of applied operators.

In addition, the use of a high-level language also allows the compiler to identify opportunities for optimization that might have been ignored by an inexperienced programmer. At the same time, the Pig environment allows developers to create new user defined functions (UDFs) that can subsequently be incorporated into developed programs.

7.10 MAHOUT

Attempting to use big data for analytics would be limited without any analytics capabilities. Mahout is a project to provide a library of

[5]See <http://pig.apache.org/>.

Table 7.1 Variables to Consider When Framing Big Data Environment		
Variable	**Intent**	**Technical Requirements**
Predisposition to parallelization	Number and type of processing node(s)	Number or processors Types of processors
Size of data to be persistently stored	Amount and allocation of disk space for distributed file system	Size of disk drives
		Number of disk drives
		Type of drives (SSD versus magnetic versus optical)
		Bus configuration (shared everything versus shared nothing, for example)
Amount of data to be accessible in memory	Amount and allocation of core memory	Amount of RAM memory Cache memories
Need for cross-node communication	Optimize speed and bandwidth	Network/cabinet configuration
		Network speed
		Network bandwidth
Types of data organization	Data management requirements	File management organization
		Database requirements
		Data orientation (row versus column)
		Type of data structures
Developer skill set	Development tools	Types of programming tools, compilers, execution models, debuggers, etc.
Types of algorithms	Analytic functionality requirements	Data warehouse/marts for OLAP Data mining and predictive analytics

scalable implementations of machine learning algorithms on top of MapReduce and Hadoop. As is described at the project's home page[6], Mahout's library includes numerous well-known analysis methods including:

- **Collaborative filtering and other user and item-based recommender algorithms,** which is used to make predictions about an individual's interest or preferences through comparison with a multitude of others that may or may not share similar characteristics.
- **Clustering,** including K-Means, Fuzzy K-Means, Mean Shift, and Dirichlet process clustering algorithms to look for groups, patterns, and commonality among selected cohorts in a population.
- **Categorization** using Naïve Bayes or decision forests to place items into already defined categories.

[6]See <http://mahout.apache.org/>.

- **Text mining** and topic modeling algorithms for scanning text and assigning contextual meanings.
- **Frequent pattern mining**, which is used for market basket analysis, comparative health analytics, and other patterns of correlation within large datasets.

Mahout also supports other methods and algorithms. The availability of implemented libraries for these types of analytics free the development team to consider the types of problems to be analyzed and more specifically, the types of analytical models that can be applied to seek the best answers.

7.11 CONSIDERATIONS

Big data analytics applications employ a variety of tools and techniques for implementation. When organizing your thoughts about developing those applications, it is important to think about the parameters that will frame your needs for technology evaluation and acquisition, sizing and configuration, methods of data organization, and required algorithms to be used or developed from scratch.

Prior to diving directly into downloading and installing software, focus on the types of big data business applications and their corresponding performance scaling needs, such as those listed in Table 7.1.

The technical requirements will guide both the hardware and the software configurations. This also allows you to align the development of the platform with the business application development needs.

7.12 THOUGHT EXERCISES

When considering the types of tools and technologies necessary to flesh out a big data application development and implementation ecosystem, here are some questions and exercises to ponder:

- For a selected big data application, describe how the process can be divided up into "chunks of work" to be performed by the pool of processors.
- Why is it a good idea for the processing nodes to work on data at colocated data nodes?

- Review the Hadoop components described in this chapter—discuss whether they will or won't adequately address your big data needs.
- Is there a value proposition for solely using HDFS as a scalable data storage option? How does this compare to a traditional storage solution in cost, security, and availability?

CHAPTER 8

Developing Big Data Applications

As we discussed in Chapter 6, most big data appliances (both hardware and software) use a collection of computing resources, typically a combination of processing nodes and storage nodes. The ability to achieve scalability to accommodate growing data volumes is predicated on multiprocessing—distributing the computation across the collection of computing nodes in ways that are aligned with the distribution of data across the storage nodes. In this chapter, we look at some of the underlying issues in enabling developers and analysts to design, build, and execute high-performance applications for big data analytics.

8.1 PARALLELISM

More precisely, one of the key objectives of using a multiprocessing node environment is to speed application execution by breaking up large "chunks" of work into much smaller ones that can be farmed out to a pool of available processing nodes. In the best of all possible worlds, the datasets to be consumed and analyzed are also distributed across a pool of storage nodes. As long as there are no dependencies forcing any one specific task to wait to begin until another specific one ends, these smaller tasks can be executed at the same time—this is the essence of what is called "task parallelism."

As an example, consider a telecommunications company that would like to market bundled mobile telecommunication services to a particular segment of households in which high school age children are transitioning to college and might be targeted for additional services at their future college locations. Part of the analysis involves looking for certain kinds of patterns among collections of call detail records among household members for households that fit the target model of the marketing campaign. The next step would be to look for other households who are transitioning into the target model and determine their suitability for the program. This is a good example of a big data analysis application that needs to scan millions, if not billions, of call detail records to look for and then match against different sets of patterns. The collections of call detail records can be "batched" into smaller sets and analyzed in parallel for intermediate results, which can later be aggregated to provide the desired insight.

8.2 THE MYTH OF SIMPLE SCALABILITY

One misconception of the big data phenomenon is the expectation of easily achievable scalable high performance resulting from automated task parallelism. One would expect that this telecommunications analysis example application would run significantly faster over larger volumes of records when it can be deployed in a big data environment. In fact, it is the concept of "automated scalability" leading to vastly increased performance that has inspired such a great interest in the power of big data analytics.

And yet, it is not so simple to achieve these performance speedups. In general, one cannot assume that any arbitrarily chosen business application can be migrated to a big data platform, recompiled, and magically scale-up in both execution speed and support for massive data volumes. Having determined that the business challenge is suited to a big data solution, the programmers have to envision a method by which the problem can be solved and design and develop the algorithms for making it happen.

8.3 THE APPLICATION DEVELOPMENT FRAMEWORK

This means that for any target big data platform, you must have an *application development framework* that supports a system development life cycle, provide a means for loading and executing the developed application, and essentially "train" the developer team to be aware of the best ways to take advantage of multiprocessor computing. A good development framework will simplify the process of developing, executing, testing, and debugging new application code, and this framework should include:

- a programming model and development tools;
- facility for program loading, execution, and for process and thread scheduling;
- system configuration and management tools.

The context for all of these framework components is tightly coupled with the key characteristics of a big data application—algorithms that take advantage of running lots of tasks in parallel on many computing nodes to analyze lots of data distributed among many storage nodes. Typically, a big data platform will consist of a collection (or a "pool") of processing nodes; the optimal performances can be achieved when all the processing nodes are kept busy, and that means maintaining a healthy allocation of tasks to idle nodes within the pool.

Any big application that is to be developed must map to this context, and that is where the programming model comes in. The programming model essentially describes two aspects of application execution within a parallel environment:

1. how an application is coded;
2. how that code maps to the parallel environment.

8.4 THE MAPREDUCE PROGRAMMING MODEL

We can use the Hadoop MapReduce programming model as an example. One can read more about MapReduce at Apache's MapReduce Tutorial Page.[1] Note that MapReduce, which can be used to develop applications to read, analyze, transform, and share massive amounts of data is not a database system but rather is a programming model introduced and described by Google researchers for parallel, distributed computation involving massive datasets (ranging from hundreds of terabytes to petabytes).

Application development in MapReduce is a combination of the familiar procedural/imperative approaches used by Java or C++ programmers embedded within what is effectively a functional language programming model such as the one used within languages like Lisp and APL. The similarity is based on MapReduce's dependence on two basic operations that are applied to sets or lists of data value pairs:

1. *Map*, which describes the computation or analysis applied to a set of input key/value pairs to produce a set of intermediate key/value pairs.

[1]See <http://hadoop.apache.org/docs/stable/mapred_tutorial.html> .

2. *Reduce*, in which the set of values associated with the intermediate key/value pairs output by the *Map* operation are combined to provide the results.

A MapReduce application is envisioned as a series of basic operations applied in a sequence to small sets of many (millions, billions, or even more) data items. These data items are logically organized in a way that enables the MapReduce execution model to allocate tasks that can be executed in parallel. The data items are indexed using a defined key into <**key, value** > pairs, in which the **key** represents some grouping criterion associated with a computed **value**. With some applications applied to massive datasets, the theory is that the computations applied during the *Map* phase to each input key/value pair are independent from one another. Figure 8.1 shows how Map and Reduce work.

Combining both data and computational independence means that both the data and the computations can be distributed across multiple storage and processing units and automatically parallelized. This

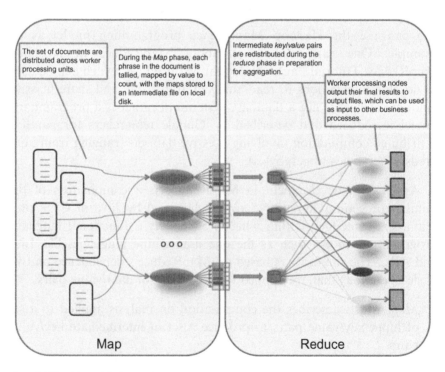

Figure 8.1 How Map and Reduce work.

parallelizability allows the programmer to exploit scalable massively parallel processing resources for increased processing speed and performance.

8.5 A SIMPLE EXAMPLE

In the canonical MapReduce example of counting the number of occurrences of a word across a corpus of many documents, the **key** is the word and the **value** is the number of times the word is counted at each process node. The process can be subdivided into much smaller sets of tasks. For example:

- The total number of occurrences of each word in the entire collection of documents is equal to the sum of the occurrences of each word in each document.
- The total number of occurrences of each word in each document can be computed as the sum of the occurrences of each word in each paragraph.
- The total number of occurrences of each word in each paragraph can be computed as the sum of the occurrences of each word in each sentence.

In this example, the determination of the right level of parallelism can be scaled in relation to the size of the "chunk" to be processed and the number of computing resources available in the pool. A single task might consist of counting the number of occurrences of each word in a single document, or a paragraph, or a sentence, depending on the level of granularity. Each time a processing node is assigned a set of tasks in processing different subsets of the data, it maintains interim results associated with each key. This will be done for all of the documents, and interim results for each word are created. Once all the interim results are completed, they can be redistributed so that all the interim results associated with a key can be assigned to a specific processing node that accumulates the results into a final result.

8.6 MORE ON MAP REDUCE

From a functional perspective, the programmer's goal is to ultimately map each word to its number of occurrences in all of the documents. This suggests the context for both the *Map* function, which allocates a data chunk to a processing node and then asks each processing node to map each word to its count, and the *Reduce* function, which collects the interim results from all the processing nodes and sorts and aggregates them to get the final results.

Under the right circumstances, the ability to create many smaller tasks that can execute in parallel allows you to take advantage of existing processing capacity and to speedup the delivery of the results. This speedup can be scaled as the data volumes to be processed increase by adding additional processing nodes and storage nodes.

Generally, the basic steps are simple, and the implementation of the program is straightforward. The programmer relies on the underlying runtime system to distribute the data to be analyzed to the processing nodes, instantiate the *Map* and *Reduce* directives across the processor pool, initiate the *Map* phase, coordinate the communication of the intermediate results, initiate the *Reduce* phase, and then collect and collate the final results. More discretely, the MapReduce programming model consists of five basic operations:

1. Input data, in which the data is loaded into the environment and is distributed across the storage nodes, and distinct data artifacts are associated with a key value.
2. Map, in which a specific task is applied to each artifact with the interim result associated with a different key value. An analogy is that each processing node has a bucket for each key, and interim results are put into the bucket for that key.
3. Sort/shuffle, in which the interim results are sorted and redistributed so that all interim results for a specific key value are located at one single-processing node. To continue the analogy, this would be the process of delivering all the buckets for a specific key to a single delivery point.
4. Reduce, in which the interim results are accumulated into a final result.
5. Output result, where the final output is sorted.

These steps are presumed to be run in sequence, and applications developed using MapReduce often execute a series of iterations of the sequence, in which the output results from iteration n becomes the input to iteration $n + 1$. This model relies on data distribution—note that in the first step where data artifacts are distributed across the environment. If the data is already distributed (such as stored in a distributed file system), this is not necessary, and only the assignment of the key is critical. That shows how large datasets can be accommodated via distribution, and also suggests scalability is achievable by adding more storage nodes.

At the same time, the Map and Reduce steps show where the bulk of the execution parallelism comes in. During the Map phase, the same task is applied to many artifacts simultaneously, and since they are independent tasks, each one can be spawned off as an independent execution thread. The same can be said for the Reduce step as well. MapReduce is reminiscent of a functional programming model, and MapReduce applications can be developed using programming languages with library support for the execution model.

8.7 OTHER BIG DATA DEVELOPMENT FRAMEWORKS

It is valuable to point out that while Hadoop and MapReduce are relatively widely known, there are other programming models that can be used to develop big data applications. Another example of a programming model is called Enterprise Control Language, or ECL, which is a data-centric programming language for a different open source big data platform called HPCC (High-Performance Computing Cluster) that was developed by a company called Seisint that was later acquired by LexisNexis.

The HPCC environment was recently spun off into a company called HPCC Systems, and a community version of the product is available for downloading from their Web site. As opposed to the functional programming model of MapReduce, ECL is a declarative programming language that describes "what" is supposed to happen to the data, but does not specify "how" it is done.[2] The declarative approach presumes the programmer has the expectation that the compiler and execution scheme automate the parallelization of the declarative statements, which in many cases simplifies the programming process. ECL provides a collection of primitive capabilities that are typical for data analysis, such as sorting, aggregation, deduplication, as well as others. With ECL, the declarative model is the source of

---

[2]For more information about ECL, see HPCC System's documentation at <http://hpccsystems.com/community/docs/ecl-language-reference/html>.

task parallelism, in which discrete and small units of work can be farmed out to waiting processing units in a cluster and executed in parallel. With ECL, each of the programming constructs can be executed in parallel.

Both of these programming models (MapReduce and ECL) are implicitly aligned with both data distribution and task/thread parallelism, which obviates the need for the programmer to explicitly direct the determination of how tasks are configured and how they are assigned to the different processing nodes. That means that we would need the execution model to automatically transform the "logical" parallelism into real parallel tasks that can be executed as individual threads.

8.8 THE EXECUTION MODEL

Let's revisit our telecommunications example and concentrate on one small piece of the puzzle: characterizing households in terms of their degrees of connectivity by looking at the frequency of contacts in relation to the call detail records. This nominally involves two tasks. First, we must analyze the frequency of telecommunication contacts (such as telephone calls, text messages, and emails) among individuals known to belong to the same household by time and by location; second, classify those households in relation to their "degree of connectivity."

The household ID becomes the key. You may want to run this application on a cluster of 100 processing nodes, but clearly there will be many orders of magnitude more household IDs to be used as key values. How do the tens of thousands (or more) microtasks get allocated across this 100-node network?

The answer is that the **execution model** effectively manages the workloads. First, when the datasets are loaded, they will be distributed across the different storage nodes available within the system configuration. There are different configurations in which storage nodes are accessible to the processing nodes, with different access methods and corresponding access times.

As we discussed in Chapter 6, often storage nodes will be directly connected to processing nodes. When the processing node is co-located at the storage node, it simplifies this allocation of tasks. The task manager also arranges for the scheduling of tasks (i.e., the order in which they are executed) and may also continuously monitor the status of each task to ensure that progress is being made. This basic approach is adapted in different ways by the developers of the execution model to support the corresponding programming model. As an example, one task manager process maintains the list of tasks to be performed and doles out those tasks based on data locality (in which the processor closest to the storage node is selected) to minimize the time associated with data latency, which slows down the computing process.

The last part of making a developed application executable is the system configuration. Again, each of the programming models must provide a way to notify the execution model the details of the execution environment: things like whether the program is being run on a single node (as might be done during the development and testing phase of development) or on a cluster, the number of nodes in a cluster, the number of storage nodes, the type of data, as well as suggestions for optimizing the shuffle or data exchange phase in which interim results are broadcast to their next processing step.

At the high level, these concepts are straightforward. The devil is in the details, and it behooves anyone considering employing a big data development framework such as Hadoop and MapReduce be properly trained in awareness of the different facets of parallel and distributed programming and how they can impact performance. Acquiring this knowledge will help in understanding the simplicity of the model and how it can be effectively used.

8.9 THOUGHT EXERCISES

When considering the application development framework for big data analytics, here are some questions and exercises to ponder:

- For each of your three most typical big data applications within your organization, describe two different ways of breaking the problem into much smaller tasks.
- Discuss how the number of tasks is related to the amount of work performed by each task. Is it better to have more tasks with smaller amounts of work or larger tasks with larger amounts of work? Why?
- What types of applications have data distributions that are not well suited to parallel execution? Why?

CHAPTER 9

NoSQL Data Management for Big Data

9.1 WHAT IS NOSQL?

In Chapter 6, we discussed different kinds of high-performance appliances from both the architectural perspective and from a data organization perspective. To continue the discussion of application development, it is valuable to continue to review the different means for managing and organizing massive data volumes to meet business needs, and in this chapter, we will look at some alternative methods for data management.

In any environment that already depends on a relational database model and/or a data warehousing approach to data management, it would be unwise to ignore support for these traditional data organizations for data that is to be implemented in a big data environment. Fortunately, most hardware and software appliances support standard approaches to standard, SQL-based relational database management systems (RDBMSs). Software appliances often bundle their execution engines with the RDBMS and utilities for creating the database structures and for bulk data loading.

However, the availability of a high-performance, elastic distributed data environment enables creative algorithms to exploit variant modes of data management in different ways. In fact, some algorithms will not be able to consume data in traditional RDBMS systems and will be acutely dependent on alternative means for data management. Many of these alternate data management frameworks are bundled under the term "NoSQL databases." The term "NoSQL" may convey two different connotations—one implying that the data management system is **not** an SQL-compliant one, while the more accepted implication is that the term means "Not only SQL," suggesting environments that combine traditional SQL (or SQL-like query languages) with alternative means of querying and access.

9.2 "SCHEMA-LESS MODELS": INCREASING FLEXIBILITY FOR DATA MANIPULATION

NoSQL data systems hold out the promise of greater flexibility in database management while reducing the dependence on more formal database administration. NoSQL databases have more relaxed modeling constraints, which may benefit both the application developer and the end-user analysts when their interactive analyses are not throttled by the need to cast each query in terms of a relational table-based environment.

Different NoSQL frameworks are optimized for different types of analyses. For example, some are implemented as key–value stores, which nicely align to certain big data programming models, while another emerging model is a graph database, in which a graph abstraction is implemented to embed both semantics and connectivity within its structure. In fact, the general concepts for NoSQL include **schema-less modeling** in which the semantics of the data are embedded within a flexible connectivity and storage model; this provides for automatic distribution of data and elasticity with respect to the use of computing, storage, and network bandwidth in ways that don't force specific binding of data to be persistently stored in particular physical locations. NoSQL databases also provide for integrated data caching that helps reduce data access latency and speed performance.

The loosening of the relational structure is intended to allow different models to be adapted to specific types of analyses. The technologies are evolving and maturing. And because of the "relaxed" approach to modeling and management that does not enforce shoehorning data into strictly defined relational structures, the models themselves do not necessarily impose any validity rules; this potentially introduces risks associated with ungoverned data management activities such as inadvertent inconsistent data replication, reinterpretation of semantics, and currency and timeliness issues.

9.3 KEY–VALUE STORES

A relatively simple type of NoSQL data store is a **key–value store**, a schema-less model in which values (or sets of values, or even more complex entity objects) are associated with distinct character strings called **keys**. Programmers may see similarity with the data structure known as a **hash table**. Other alternative NoSQL data stores are variations on the key–value theme, which lends a degree of credibility to the model.

As an example, consider the data subset represented in Table 9.1. The *key* is the name of the automobile make, while the *value* is a list of names of models associated with that automobile make.

As can be inferred from the example, the key–value store does not impose any constraints about data typing or data structure—the value associated with the key is the value, and it is up to the consuming business applications to assert expectations about the data values and their semantics and interpretation. This demonstrates the schema-less property of the model.

The core operations performed on a key–value store include:

- Get(*key*), which returns the value associated with the provided *key*.
- Put(*key, value*), which associates the *value* with the *key*.
- Multi-get(*key1, key2,..., keyN*), which returns the list of values associated with the list of *keys*.
- Delete(*key*), which removes the entry for the *key* from the data store.

One critical characteristic of a key–value store is uniqueness of the key—to find the values you are looking for, you must use the exact key. In this data management approach, if you want to associate multiple values with a single key, you need to consider the representations of the objects and how they are associated with the key. For example, you may want to associate a list of attributes with a single key, which may suggest that the value stored with the key is yet another key–value store object itself.

Key–value stores are essentially very long, and presumably thin tables (in that there are not many columns associated with each row). The table's rows can be sorted by the key value to simplify finding the

Table 9.1 Example Data Represented in a Key–Value Store	
Key	Value
...	
"BMW"	{"1-Series", "3-Series", "5-Series", "5-Series GT", "7-Series", "X3", "X5", "X6", "Z4"}
"Buick"	{"Enclave", "LaCrosse", "Lucerne", "Regal"}
"Cadillac"	{"CTS", "DTS", "Escalade", "Escalade ESV", "Escalade EXT", "SRX", "STS"}
...	

key during a query. Alternatively, the keys can be *hashed* using a hash function that maps the key to a particular location (sometimes called a "bucket") in the table. Additional supporting data structures and algorithms (such as bit vectors and bloom filters) can be used to even determine whether the key exists in the data set at all. The representation can grow indefinitely, which makes it good for storing large amounts of data that can be accessed relatively quickly, as well as environments requiring incremental appends of data. Examples include capturing system transaction logs, managing profile data about individuals, or maintaining access counts for millions of unique web page URLs.

The simplicity of the representation allows massive amounts of indexed data values to be appended to the same key–value table, which can then be *sharded*, or distributed across the storage nodes. Under the right conditions, the table is distributed in a way that is aligned with the way the keys are organized, so that the hashing function that is used to determine where any specific key exists in the table can also be used to determine which node holds that key's bucket (i.e., the portion of the table holding that key).

While key–value pairs are very useful for both storing the results of analytical algorithms (such as phrase counts among massive numbers of documents) and for producing those results for reports, the model does pose some potential drawbacks. One is that the model will not inherently provide any kind of traditional database capabilities (such as atomicity of transactions, or consistency when multiple transactions are executed simultaneously)—those capabilities must be provided by the application itself. Another is that as the model grows, maintaining unique values as keys may become more difficult, requiring the introduction of some complexity in generating character strings that will remain unique among a myriad of keys.

9.4 DOCUMENT STORES

A document store is similar to a key–value store in that stored objects are associated (and therefore accessed via) character string keys. The difference is that the values being stored, which are referred to as "documents," provide some structure and encoding of the managed data. There are different common encodings, including XML (Extensible Markup Language), JSON (Java Script Object Notation), BSON (which is a binary encoding of JSON objects), or other means of serializing data (i.e., packaging up the potentially linearizing data values associated with a data record or object).

As an example, in Figure 9.1 we have some examples of documents stored in association with the names of specific retail locations. Note that while the three examples all represent locations, yet the representative models differ. The document representation embeds the model so that the meanings of the document values can be inferred by the application.

One of the differences between a key–value store and a document store is that while the former requires the use of a key to retrieve data, the latter often provides a means (either through a programming API or using a query language) for querying the data based on the contents. Because the approaches used for encoding the documents embed the object metadata, one can use methods for querying by example. For instance, using the example in Figure 9.1, one could execute a FIND (MallLocation: "Westfield Wheaton") that would pull out all documents associated with the Retail Stores in that particular shopping mall.

9.5 TABULAR STORES

Tabular, or table-based stores are largely descended from Google's original Bigtable design[1] to manage structured data. The HBase model described in Chapter 7 is an example of a Hadoop-related NoSQL data management system that evolved from bigtable.

The bigtable NoSQL model allows sparse data to be stored in a three-dimensional table that is indexed by a row key (that is used in a fashion that is similar to the key–value and document stores), a column key that indicates the specific attribute for which a data value is stored, and a timestamp that may refer to the time at which the row's column value was stored.

As an example, various attributes of a web page can be associated with the web page's URL: the HTML content of the page, URLs of other web pages that link to this web page, and the author of the content. Columns in a Bigtable model are grouped together as "families,"

[1]Chang F, Dean J, Ghemawat S, Hsieh WC, Wallach DA, Burrows M, et al. Bigtable: a distributed storage system for structured data. Accessed via <http://research.google.com/archive/bigtable.html> (Last accessed 08-08-13).

```
{StoreName:"Retail Store #34",
 {Street:"1203 O ST", City:"Lincoln", State:"NE", ZIP:"68508"}
 }

{StoreName:"Retail Store #65",
 {MallLocation:"Westfield Wheaton", City:"Wheaton", State:"IL"}
 }

{StoreName:"Retail Store $102",
 {Latitude:" 40.748328", Longitude:" -73.985560"}
 }
```

Figure 9.1 Example of document store.

and the timestamps enable management of multiple versions of an object. The timestamp can be used to maintain history—each time the content changes, new column affiliations can be created with the timestamp of when the content was downloaded.

9.6 OBJECT DATA STORES

In some ways, object data stores and object databases seem to bridge the worlds of schema-less data management and the traditional relational models. On the one hand, approaches to object databases can be similar to document stores except that the document stores explicitly serializes the object so the data values are stored as strings, while object databases maintain the object structures as they are bound to object-oriented programming languages such as C++, Objective-C, Java, and Smalltalk. On the other hand, object database management systems are more likely to provide traditional ACID (atomicity, consistency, isolation, and durability) compliance—characteristics that are bound to database reliability. Object databases are not relational databases and are not queried using SQL.

9.7 GRAPH DATABASES

Graph databases provide a model of representing individual entities and numerous kinds of relationships that connect those entities. More precisely, it employs the graph abstraction for representing connectivity, consisting of a collection of *vertices* (which are also referred to as *nodes* or *points*) that represent the modeled entities, connected by *edges* (which are also referred to as *links*, *connections*, or *relationships*) that capture the way that two entities are related. Graph analytics performed on graph data stores are somewhat different than more frequently used querying and reporting, and we cover graph databases in much greater detail in Chapter 10.

9.8 CONSIDERATIONS

The decision to use a NoSQL data store instead of a relational model must be aligned with the data consumers' expectations for compliance with their expectations of relational models. As should be apparent, many NoSQL data management environments are engineered for two key criteria:

1. fast accessibility, whether that means inserting data into the model or pulling it out via some query or access method;
2. scalability for volume, so as to support the accumulation and management of massive amounts of data.

The different approaches are amenable to extensibility, scalability, and distribution, and these characteristics blend nicely with programming models (like MapReduce) with straightforward creation and execution of many parallel processing threads. Distributing a tabular data store or a key—value store allows many queries/accesses to be performed simultaneously, especially when the hashing of the keys maps to different data storage nodes. Employing different data allocation strategies will allow the tables to grow indefinitely without requiring significant rebalancing.

In other words, these data organizations are designed for high-performance computing for reporting and analysis. However, most NoSQL environments are not generally designed for transaction processing, and it would require some whittling down of the list of vendors to find those that support ACID transactions.

9.9 THOUGHT EXERCISES

When considering NoSQL data stores, here are some questions and exercises to ponder:

- At what point do you decide that a traditional RDBMS implemented on a standard server environment is insufficient to satisfy the business needs of an analytical application?

- For the most valuable big data opportunity in your organization, describe how the data would be mapped to a key–value store model, a document store model, and a tabular model.
- Would you consider using any of these approaches to replace existing production data management applications? Why?
- Describe a pilot application that uses one of the NoSQL approaches described in this chapter.

CHAPTER 10

Using Graph Analytics for Big Data

While we have discussed how the various techniques and technologies for big data appliances can increase performance (in terms of scalability for computation speed or for data volumes), we have also seen that the ways that certain applications are mapped to a typical big data stack might have limitations in scalability due to memory access latency or network bandwidth. Yet the promise of big data must go beyond increased scalability for known problems.

Big data analytics systems should enable a platform that can support different analytics techniques that can be adapted in ways that help solve a variety of challenging problems. This suggests that these systems are high performance, elastic distributed data environments that enable the use of creative algorithms to exploit variant modes of data management in ways that differ from the traditional batch-oriented approach of traditional approaches to data warehousing.

In this chapter, we look at graph analytics, which is an analytics alternative that uses an abstraction called a **graph model**. The simplicity of this model allows for rapidly absorbing and connecting large volumes of data from many sources in ways that finesse limitations of the source structures (or lack thereof, of course). Graph analytics is an alternative to the traditional data warehouse model as a framework for absorbing both structured and unstructured data from various sources to enable analysts to probe the data in an undirected manner.

As we will see, the graph model allows you to tightly couple the meaning of entity relationships as part of the representation of the relationship. This effectively embeds the semantics of relationships among different entities within the structure, providing an ability to both invoke traditional-style queries (to answer typical "search" queries modeled after known patterns) and enable more sophisticated undirected analyses. These undirected "discovery" analyses, include inferencing, identification of interesting patterns, and application of deduction, all using an iterative approach that analysts can use to discover actionable knowledge that was previously unknown. This allows the analysts to rapidly seek out emerging patterns and enable real-time knowledge-driven decision making in the context of how these newly discovered patterns impact the corporate business value drivers.

10.1 WHAT IS GRAPH ANALYTICS?

It is worth delving somewhat into the graph model and the methods used for managing and manipulating graphs:

- What constitutes graph analytics?
- Types of problems that are suited to graph analytics.
- Types of questions that are addressed using graph analytics.
- Types of graphs that are commonly encountered.
- The degree of prevalence within big data analytics problems.

This motivates an understanding of its utility and flexibility for discovery-style analysis in relation to specific types of business problems, how common those types of problems are, and why they are nicely abstracted to the graph model. In addition, we will discuss the challenges of attempting to execute graph analytics on conventional hardware and consider aspects of specialty platforms that can help in achieving the right level of scalability and performance.

10.2 THE SIMPLICITY OF THE GRAPH MODEL

Graph analytics is based on a model of representing individual entities and numerous kinds of relationships that connect those entities. More precisely, it employs the graph abstraction for representing connectivity, consisting of a collection of *vertices* (which are also referred to as *nodes* or *points*) that represent the modeled entities, connected by *edges* (which are also referred to as *links, connections,* or *relationships*) that capture the way that two entities are related.

Some simple examples are shown in Figure 10.1.

The flexibility of the model is based on its simplicity. A simple unlabeled undirected graph, in which the edges between vertices neither reflect the nature of the relationship nor indicate their direction, has limited utility. But, as we see in the examples in Figure 10.1, adding context by labeling the vertices and edges enhances the meanings embedded within the graph, and by extension, the entire representation of a network.

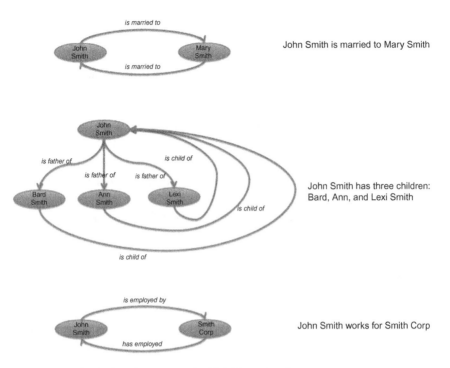

John Smith is married to Mary Smith

John Smith has three children: Bard, Ann, and Lexi Smith

John Smith works for Smith Corp

Figure 10.1 Examples of relationships represented as labeled directed graphs.

Among other enhancements, these can enrich the meaning of the nodes and edges represented in the graph model:

- Vertices can be labeled to indicate the types of entities that are related.
- Edges can be labeled with the nature of the relationship.
- Edges can be directed to indicate the "flow" of the relationship.
- Weights can be added to the relationships represented by the edges.
- Additional properties can be attributed to both edges and vertices.
- Multiple edges can reflect multiple relationships between pairs of vertices.

10.3 REPRESENTATION AS TRIPLES

In essence, these enhancements help in building a semantic graph—a directed graph that can be represented using a *triple* format consisting of a *subject* (the source point of the relationship), an *object* (the target), and a *predicate* (that models the type of the relationship).

The same examples in Figure 10.1 could be modeled as a set of triples, as shown in Table 10.1.

A collection of these triples is called a semantic database, and this kind of database can capture additional properties of each triple relationship as attributes of the triple. Almost any type of entity and relationship can be represented in a graph model, which means two key things: the process of adding new entities and relationships is not impeded when new datasets are to be included, with new types of entities and connections to be incorporated, and the model is particularly suited to types of discovery analytics that seek out new patterns embedded within the graph that are of critical business interest.

10.4 GRAPHS AND NETWORK ORGANIZATION

The concept of the social network has been around for many years, and in recent times has been materialized as communities in which individual entities create online personas and connect and interact with others within the community. Yet the idea of the social network extends beyond specific online implementations, and encompasses a wide variety of example environments that directly map to the graph model. That being said, one of the benefits of the graph model is the ability to detect patterns or organization that are inherent within the represented network, such as:

- **Embedded micronetworks**: Looking for small collections of entities that form embedded "microcommunities." Some examples include determining the originating sources for a hot new purchasing trend,

Table 10.1 Triples Derived from the Example in Figure 10.1		
Subject	Predicate	Object
John Smith	Is married to	Mary Smith
Mary Smith	Is married to	John Smith
John Smith	Is father of	Brad Smith
John Smith	Is father of	Ann Smith
John Smith	Is father of	Lexi Smith
Brad Smith	Is child of	John Smith
Ann Smith	Is child of	John Smith
Lexi Smith	Is child of	John Smith
John Smith	Is employed by	Smith Corp
Smith Corp	Has employed	John Smith

identifying a terrorist cell based on patterns of communication across a broad swath of call detail records, or sets of individuals within a particular tiny geographic region with similar political views.

- **Communication models**: Modeling communication across a community triggered by a specific event, such as monitoring the "buzz" across a social media channel associated with the rumored release of a new product, evaluating best methods for communicating news releases, or correlation between travel delays and increased mobile telephony activity.
- **Collaborative communities**: Isolating groups of individuals that share similar interests, such as groups of health care professionals working in the same area of specialty, purchasers with similar product tastes, or individuals with a precise set of employment skills.
- **Influence modeling**: Looking for entities holding influential positions within a network for intermittent periods of time, such as computer nodes that have been hijacked and put to work as proxies for distributed denial of service attacks or for emerging cybersecurity threats, or individuals that are recognized as authorities within a particular area.
- **Distance modeling**: Analyzing the distances between sets of entities, such as looking for strong correlations between occurrences of sets of statistically improbable phrases among large sets of search engines queries, or the amount of effort necessary to propagate a message among a set of different communities.

Each of these example applications is a discovery analysis that looks for patterns that are not known in advance. As a result, these are less suited to pattern searches form relational database systems, such as a data warehouse or data mart, and are better suited to a more dynamic representation like the graph model.

10.5 CHOOSING GRAPH ANALYTICS

Deciding the appropriateness of an analytics application to a graph analytics solution instead of the other big data alternatives can be based on these characteristics and factors of business problems:

- **Connectivity**: The solution to the business problem requires the analysis of relationships and connectivity between a variety of different types of entities.

- **Undirected discovery**: Solving the business problem involves iterative undirected analysis to seek out as-of-yet unidentified patterns.
- **Absence of structure**: Multiple datasets to be subjected to the analysis are provided without any inherent imposed structure.
- **Flexible semantics**: The business problem exhibits dependence on contextual semantics that can be attributed to the connections and corresponding relationships.
- **Extensibility**: Because additional data can add to the knowledge embedded within the graph, there is a need for the ability to quickly add in new data sources or streaming data as needed for further interactive analysis.
- **Knowledge is embedded in the network**: Solving the business problem involves the ability to exploit critical features of the embedded relationships that can be inferred from the provided data.
- **Ad hoc nature of the analysis**: There is a need to run ad hoc queries to follow lines of reasoning.
- **Predictable interactive performance**: The ad hoc nature of the analysis creates a need for high performance because discovery in big data is a collaborative man/machine undertaking, and predictability is critical when the results are used for operational decision making.

10.6 GRAPH ANALYTICS USE CASES

Having reviewed the business problems that are suited to using a solution based on a graph analytics model, we can examine some use cases for graph analytics. In these scenarios, we look at the business problem, why the traditional approach may not be optimal, and then discuss how the graph analytics approach is best suited to solving the business challenges.

Some example business applications that are aligned with these criteria include:

- **Health care quality analytics**, in which patient health encounter histories, diagnoses, procedures, treatment approaches, and results of clinical trials contribute to the ability to analyze the comparative effectiveness of different health care options. The process requires the absorption of many different collections of medical histories, clinical records, laboratory results, and prescription records from many different sources and systems. In turn, the application must guide health care providers in a timely and efficient manner by enabling the rapid assessment of therapies used for other patients with similar characteristics (such as age, clinical history, and associated risk factors) that have the most positive outcomes. This analysis creates a graph representing the corresponding relationships and may also combine health histories with additional data sources that can be easily integrated into the existing graph model.

- **Concept-based correlations** that seek to organize large bodies of knowledge. Some examples include looking for contextual relationships between scientific health care research and particular types of pharmaceuticals, investigative journalists seeking connections among individuals referred to in a variety of news sources, fraud analysts evaluating financial irregularities across multiple-related organizations, or even correlations between corporate behavior and increased health risks. Each of these examples involve the absorption of many content artifacts from multiple varied data sources, the need to combine isolated pieces of information extracted from among the corpus of documents, and a discovery activity looking for correlations that are currently hidden or unknown.

- **Cybersecurity**: The numbers of cyber attacks are increasing, and their sophistication is expanding way beyond distributed denial of service (DDoS), which is more frequently being used as a premise and distraction while more insidious attacks seek to traverse corporate firewalls, extract critical business information, or incrementally drain individual financial accounts while operating completely under the radar. Monitoring for cybersecurity events is a process in which a wide variety of massive streaming datasets (such as network logs, NetFlow, DNS, and IDS data) need to be rapidly captured and integrated into a model that allows for both identification of known attack patterns as well as the discovery of new patterns that emerge as the attacks become more elaborate. A graph analytics approach can address the challenge by capturing and loading the entire volume and breadth of the available datasets coupled with an evolving model that can quickly log connections and relationships that is used to identify new patterns of attack. This graph-based approach allows analysts to rapidly get results from many ad hoc queries requested from a model managing massive amounts of data representing thousands of interconnected entities. This approach enables the analysts to quickly identify potential cyber-threats in minutes, or even seconds so that defensive actions can be taken quickly.

10.7 GRAPH ANALYTICS ALGORITHMS AND SOLUTION APPROACHES

The graph model is inherently suited to enable a broad range of analyses that are generally unavailable to users of a standard data warehouse framework. As suggested by these examples, instead of just providing reports or enabling online analytical processing (OLAP) systems, graph analytics applications employ algorithms that traverse or analyze graphs to detect and potentially identify interesting patterns that are sentinels for business opportunities for increasing revenue, identifying security risks, detecting fraud, waste, or abuse, financial trading signals, or even looking for optimal individualized health care treatments. Some of the types of analytics algorithmic approaches include:

- **Community and network analysis**, in which the graph structures are traversed in search of groups of entities connected in particularly "close" ways. One example is a collection of entities that are completely connected (i.e., each member of the set is connected to all other members of the set).
- **Path analysis**, which analyze the shapes and distances of the different paths that connect entities within the graph.
- **Clustering**, which examines the properties of the vertices and edges to identify characteristics of entities that can be used to group them together.
- **Pattern detection and pattern analysis**, or methods for identifying anomalous or unexpected patterns requiring further investigation.
- **Probabilistic graphical models** such as Bayesian networks or Markov networks for various application such as medical diagnosis, protein structure prediction, speech recognition, or assessment of default risk for credit applications.
- **Graph metrics** that are applied to measurements associated with the network itself, including the degree of the vertices (i.e., the number of edges in and out of the vertex), or centrality and distance (including the degree to which particular vertices are "centrally located" in the graph, or how close vertices are to each other based on the length of the paths between them).

These graph analytic algorithms can yield interesting patterns that might go undetected in a data warehouse model, and these patterns themselves can become the templates or models for new searches. In other words, the graph analytics approach can satisfy both the discovery and the use of patterns typically used for analysis and reporting.

10.8 TECHNICAL COMPLEXITY OF ANALYZING GRAPHS

As more use cases similar to the ones shared in this chapter emerge that are expected to consume and analyze massive datasets, the question of performance gradually stands out as one of the potential barriers to success. To what extent do big data platforms effectively satisfy the demand for high performance? Answering that question requires a better understanding of some of the complexities of graph analytics problems and topologies.

There are some characteristics of graphs that inhibit the ability of typical computing platforms to provide the rapid responses or satisfy the need for scalability, especially as data volumes continue to explode. Some of the factors that might introduce performance penalties that are not easily addressed on standard hardware architectures include:

- **Unpredictability of graph memory accesses**: The types of discovery analyses in graph analytics often require the simultaneous traversal of multiple paths within a network to find the interesting patterns for further review or optimal solutions to a problem. The graph model is represented using data structures that incorporate the links between the represented entities, and this differs substantially from a traditional database model. In a parallel environment, many traversals can be triggered at the same time, but each graph traversal is inherently dependent on the ability to follow the links from the subject to the target in the representation. Unlike queries to structured databases, the memory access patterns are not predictable, limiting the ability to reduce data access latency by efficiently streaming prefetched data through the different levels of the memory hierarchy, as briefly discussed in Chapter 6. Much execution time is spent accessing memory, while the processors wait for the memory accesses to complete.
- **Graph growth models**: As more information is introduced into an environment, real-world networks grow in an interesting way. The larger the graph becomes, the more it exhibits what is called "preferential connectivity"—newly introduced entities are more likely to

connect to already existing ones, and existing nodes with a high degree of connectivity are more likely to continue to be "popular" in that they will continue to attract new connections. This means that graphs continue to grow, but apparently that growth does not scale equally across the data structure.

- **Dynamic interactions with graphs**: As with any big data application, graphs to be analyzed are populated from a wide variety of data sources of large or massive data volumes, streamed at varying rates. But while the graph must constantly absorb many rapidly changing data streams and process the incorporation of connections and relationships into the persistent representation of the graph, the environment must also satisfy the need to rapidly respond to many simultaneous discovery analyses. Therefore, a high-performance graph analytics solution must accommodate the dynamic nature without allowing for any substantial degradation in analytics performance.

- **Complexity of graph partitioning**: Graphs tend to cluster among centers of high connectivity, as many networks naturally have "hubs" consisting of a small group of nodes with many connections. The benefit of having hubs is that in general it shortens the distances among collections of nodes in the graph. The hubs often showcase entities that may be of particular interest because of their perceived centrality. But while one of the benefits of big data platforms is the expectation of distribution of data and computation, the existence of hubs make it difficult to partition the graph among different processing units because of the multiplicity of connections. Arbitrarily distributing the data structures in ways that span or cross multiple partitions will lead to increased cross-partition network traffic, which effectively eliminates the perceived performance benefit of data distribution.

10.9 FEATURES OF A GRAPH ANALYTICS PLATFORM

If your big data challenge is suited to a graph analytics solution, it is worth enumerating some key features to look for, both from the software and from the hardware platform perspectives. These can effectively grouped into three sets of features: ease of development and implementation, interoperability with complementary reporting and analysis technologies, and system execution performance.

The ease of development features of the platform is enabled through the adoption of industry standards as well as supporting general requirements for big data applications, such as:

- **Seamless data intake**: Providing a seamless capability to easily absorb and fuse data from a variety of different sources.
- **Data integration**: A semantics-based approach is necessary for graph analytics to integrate different sets of data that do not have predetermined structure. Similar to other NoSQL approaches (as discussed in Chapter 9), the schema-less approach of the semantic model must provide the flexibility not provided by relational database models.
- **Inferencing**: The application platform should provide methods for inferencing and deduction of new information and insights derived from the embedded relationships and connectivity.
- **Standards-based representation**: Any graph analytics platform must employ the resource description framework standard (the RDF, see http://www.w3.org/RDF/) to use triples for representing the graph. Representing the graph using RDF allows for the use of the SPARQL query language standard (see http://www.w3.org/TR/rdf-sparql-query/) for executing queries against a triple-based data management environment.

Interoperability is critical, and here are some considerations for the operational aspects of the platform:

- **Workflow integration**: Providing a graph analytics platform that is segregated from the existing reporting and analytics environments will have limited value when there are gaps in incorporating results from across the different environments. Make sure that the graph analytics platform is aligned with the analysis and decision-making workflows for the associated business processes.
- **Visualization**: Presenting discoveries using visualization tools is critical to highlight their value. Look for platforms that have tight integration with visualization services.
- **"Complementariness"**: A graph analytics platform augments an organization's analytics capability and is not intended to be a replacement. Any graph analytics capabilities must complement existing data warehouses, data marts, OLAP engines, and Hadoop analytic environments.

Finally, although all of the following are reasonable expectations for any big data platform, these criteria are particularly important for graph analytics due to the nature of the representation and the types of discovery analyses performed:

- **High-speed I/O**: Meeting this expectation for real-time integration requires a scalable infrastructure, particularly with respect to high-speed I/O channels, which will speed the intake of multiple data streams and thereby support graphs that are rapidly changing as new data is absorbed.
- **High-bandwidth network**: As a significant burden of data access may cross node barriers, employing a high-speed/high-bandwidth network interconnect will also help reduce data latency delays, especially for chasing pointers across the graph.
- **Multithreading**: Fine-grained multithreading allows the simultaneous exploration of different paths and efficiently creating, managing, and allocating threads to available nodes on a massively parallel processing architecture can alleviate the challenge of predictability.
- **Large memory**: A very large memory shared across multiple processors reduces the need to partition the graph across independent environments. This helps to reduce the performance impacts associated with graph partitioning. Large memories are useful in keeping a large part, if not all of the graph resident in-memory. By migrating allocated tasks to where the data is resident in memory reduces the impact of data access latency delays.

10.10 CONSIDERATIONS: DEDICATED APPLIANCES FOR GRAPH ANALYTICS

There are different emerging methods of incorporating graph analytics into the enterprise. One class is purely a software approach, providing an ability to create, populate, and query graphs. This approach enables the necessary functionality and may provide the ease-of-implementation and deployment. Most, if not all, software implementations will use industry standards, such as RDF and SPARQL, and may even leverage complementary tools for inferencing and deduction. However, the performance of a software-only implementation is limited by its use of the available hardware, and even using commodity servers cannot necessarily enable it to natively exploit performance and optimization.

Another class is the use of a dedicated appliance for graph analytics. From an algorithmic perspective, this approach is equally capable as one that solely relies on software. However, from a performance perspective, there is no doubt that a dedicated platform will take advantage of high-performance I/O, high-bandwidth networking, in-memory computation, and native multithreading to provide the optimal performance for creating, growing, and analyzing graphs that are built from multiple high-volume data streams. Software approaches may be satisfactory for smaller graph analytics problems, but as data volumes and network complexity grow, the most effective means for return on investment may necessitate the transition to a dedicated graph analytics appliance.

10.11 THOUGHT EXERCISES

When considering graph analytics, here are some questions and exercises to ponder:

- What are the main criteria you would use to determine whether to use a structured database approach or a graph analytics approach to addressing a particular business challenge?
- Of the most valuable three big data opportunities within your organization, which are most suited to a graph analytics approach?
- Would a graph analytics platform replace any existing production business intelligence and reporting applications? If yes, why, and if not, why not?
- Describe a pilot application for graph analytics.

CHAPTER 11

Developing the Big Data Roadmap

11.1 INTRODUCTION

The goal of this book is to influence rational thinking when it comes to big data and big data analytics. Not every business problem is a big data problem, and not every big data solution is appropriate for all organizations. One benefit of rational thought is that instead of blindly diving into the deep end of the big data pool, following the guidance in this book will help frame those scenarios in which your business can (as well as help determine it cannot) benefit from big data methods and technologies. If so, the guidance should also help to clarify the evaluation criteria for scoping the acquisition and integration of technology.

This final chapter is meant to bring the presented ideas together and motivate the development of a roadmap for evaluating and potentially implementing big data within the organization. Each of the sections in this chapter can be used as a springboard for refining a more detailed task plan with specific objectives and deliverables. Hopefully, this chapter can help devise a program management approach for transitioning to an environment that effectively exploits these exciting technologies.

11.2 BRAINSTORM: ASSESS THE NEED AND VALUE OF BIG DATA

The decision to evaluate and potentially add big data technologies to the organization is informed through a collaborative process that first establishes that there is a potential need, that the need can be addressed using one or more components of the technology, and that the benefits of evaluating, developing, and deploying the technology far outweigh the costs. The first step is a needs assessment, and often that can be motivated through facilitated sessions in which the business's mission and key performance measures are considered to identify the factors to be used to assess the value proposition. Part of this task includes defining the brainstorming process and focusing on deciding what types of sessions will be done and what the expected results of the sessions will be. Some specific aspects include:

- Facilitation: What are the characteristics of the individuals facilitating these meetings? Will the sessions be facilitated using internal resources, or would it be better to engage external parties with experience in these kinds of brainstorming sessions?
- Agenda: How many sessions will there be, how will the time be allocated, and who sets the agenda? What are the expectations for what will be discussed, how are the topics selected, and what is the best balance to strike between controlled discussions and open conversations?
- Deliverables: What are the expected questions to be asked and answered? Scope those questions into alternative paths to simplify the process of reaching consensus.
- Evaluation criteria: Using the corporate value drivers and performance measures as the baseline for evaluation, specify the variables to be used to assess the value proposition. This will be a mix of potential lift (e.g., increased revenues or decreased costs) and associated resource costs (e.g., cost of technology, time to value).
- Attendees: First, determine the roles that are to be invited to the meeting and identify the specific individuals that are to be asked to attend, and then send out the invitations.
- Inputs: Identify the information that is required to be collected and then disseminated prior to the brainstorming sessions, collect that data, and publish it to the attendees.

The objective of these sessions is to determine if there is value in testing out big data as compared to the resource costs. The output is an agreement as to a value proposition that can be communicated to others in the organization.

11.3 ORGANIZATIONAL BUY-IN

As part of the technology adoption cycle to support the evaluation and adoption of big data techniques and big data analytics, it is critical to reach out to the key business process owners, information consumers, enterprise architects, technologists, and application teams to gather their support. This step is intended to identify those key individuals in the organization that need to be involved in the process of acquiring, proving, and then deploying big data solutions, and to then make them aware of their potential roles and responsibilities.

The by-product of the brainstorming sessions is a value proposition suggesting the potential benefits of implementing big data applications. The objective of this step is to communicate that value proposition so as to gain acceptance and buy-in from the key stakeholders in the form of commitment to supporting and funding the program. Perhaps one aspect of this process is a pilot or proof-of-concept project, and using the experiences gained to guide the longer term development of a program blueprint and plan. As suggested in Chapter 3, the communication plan should specify not only the intent of a pilot but should also provide a technology adoption plan that details the methods for transitioning from an experimental phase to a production design phase, including:

- identifying the need for additional resources;
- assembling a development environment;
- assembling a testing environment;
- assessing the level of effort for design, development, and implementation;
- identifying staffing requirements;
- providing a program plan for running and managing the technology in the enterprise over time.

A coherent communication plan not only frames the business user expectations but it also jump-starts the specification of a program blueprint, including some suggested alternatives approaches for deploying big data.

11.4 BUILD THE TEAM

We initially considered the appropriate roles in Chapter 3, and in review, the roles of the members of the big data application team can be organized into different categories.

The first category of roles includes the liaisons with the business. These people are either business function leaders or senior business evangelists. Some sample roles or job titles may include:

- The **business evangelist**, who has a deep knowledge of the business processes, understands core weaknesses, and is aware of any performance barriers imposed by the existing technical infrastructure. The business evangelist's skills span both the business and the technical arenas, and that person is aware of the ways that emerging or disruptive technologies can add value. The business evangelist takes on the marketing roles for big data: socializing the value proposition, exploring how business process owners can adapt their processes and applications to using a big data environment, looking for opportunities for efficiencies or improved performance, and engaging business users to solicit their input to understand their current and future needs. The business evangelist helps in guiding the selection of alternative technologies. The business evangelist must have a combination of good communication and presentation skills and deep contextual business knowledge, as well as a clear understanding of technology in general and big data techniques in particular. The person filling this role should have technical background (such as mathematics or computer science) as well as fundamental business savviness.

- The **technical evangelist**, who has an understanding of the computer science aspects of big data platforms, is aware of the details of the architecture behind big data technology and has familiarity with the business domains. This combination allows the technical evangelist to have insight into the ways that the technology can potentially improve different business applications. These improvements may include expanding the scalability of existing business processes, speeding the execution of existing business processes, improving the precision and accuracy of analytical results through increased data availability, or by enabling new capabilities that had not previously been available. The technical evangelist helps in mapping alternative technologies to the business problems, and works with the technical architects in designing approaches and selecting algorithms to apply. The technical evangelist must combine deep knowledge of technology in general and big data techniques with good communication and presentation skills, and have deep contextual business knowledge as well as fundamental knowledge of the business.

The second category of roles involves the oversight and management of the program, with some suggested titles and descriptions such as:

- **Program manager**: This role is critical for overseeing the transition from vision to reality, and requires an experienced individual with project management expertise. The program manager is charged with planning and overseeing the processes for selecting business problems to be addressed, designing the applications, configuration of the system platforms, sizing and scaling, development, and implementation. It is the program manager's job to generally ensure that the developed applications remain aligned with organizational expectations, remain within an allocated budget, and are properly documented to ensure that the best practices can be captured and migrated into production.

- **Project manager**: The project manager is the key point for managing the design and implementation of a specific big data application. The project manager will combine process development experience with technical knowledge to guide the architects and developers in mapping solutions to the big data techniques and platforms. The project manager will also be the conduit of information from the development team to the program manager, and will be expected to provide feedback about the usability and appropriateness of the selected technologies. The project manager "owns" the development schedule and is expected to ensure that the right architects, designers, and developers are brought into the project at the right times. At the same time, the project managers are expected to be "hands-on" in the development process and work with the development team to design, build, test, and implement applications.

The third category of roles includes the development practitioners, with titles and descriptions such as:

- **Big data application architect**: Because there is a need for knowledge about how traditional nonparallel/distributed applications can be redesigned to be implemented in a high-performance framework, there is a need for application architects with a firm background in parallel and distributed computing. This person is knowledgeable about fundamental performance "gotchas" that will impede the speed, scalability, and extensibility of any application requiring massive data volumes. Look for software developers and architects with application experience in high-performance computing.
- **Data integration specialist**: This individual has experience in data extraction, transformation, loading, and data transformations in preparation for cleansing and delivery to target systems. Seek people with experience with ETL tools, data federation and virtualization, data quality, and metadata analysis.

- **Platform architect**: The platform architect is responsible for assessing the functional and performance requirements for the developed application, and they must be able to scope and size the technical components of the system. This individual will have experience in building and/or configuring big data technology platforms, and they will be familiar with the performance characteristics of the different tools and programming models.
- **Application developer**: Similar to the application architect, this role requires an application developer with a background in parallel and distributed computing. Look for candidates and technical resources with the right set of skills for programming and testing parallel and distributed applications.

The fourth category includes the analysts:

- **Business analyst**: This is the person who engages with the business process owners and solicits their needs and expectations. This process identifies some of the key quantifiable measures for evaluating the business benefits of the new technology and frames the technical requirements for any pilot project. Look for individuals who combine experience in a business analyst role and who are able to effectively translate business expectations into specific data analysis results. This involves decomposition of problems into discrete analytical tasks and working in tandem with the data analysts/data scientists to develop and deploy analytical models using the developed applications and corresponding tool suites.
- **Data scientist**: This recently coined term is a modernization of the data analyst role, with the suggestion that individuals with particular skills in large-scale data analysis coupled with data mining and predictive analytics experience are primary candidates. The data scientist combines knowledge of computer science, the use of high-performance applications, and statistics, economics, mathematics, and probabilistic analysis skills. There are many opportunities for skilled data analysts to be successful in this role.

Of course, there may be other roles that will be appropriate for the team. At the same time, some of the roles suggested here might be performed by the same resource. For example, the business and technical evangelist roles might be combined, as might the data scientist and business analyst roles. This is just a starting place, and your mileage may vary.

11.5 SCOPING AND PILOTING A PROOF OF CONCEPT

The goal of a proof of concept or pilot project is to evaluate the degree to which big data technology can address identified potential business opportunities. Of course, any proof of concept must have defined performance criteria and measures based on business expectations. Those criteria will help the decision makers determine whether to commit to big data or to abandon the technology. That involves a process with some discrete steps:

1. **Specify specific business opportunity**: After collecting opinions from the business users about ways that broader access to analytics based on massive data volumes can improve their potential for business success, select one of the business opportunities to be the subject of the pilot.
2. **Specify performance criteria**: Review the performance and scalability issues, and consider the potential positive impacts of big data to the selected business application. For the pilot, define success criteria that are tied to key value drivers such as increased revenue, decreased costs, or reduced risk.
3. **Assess data requirements**: Consider some different perspectives on the information needed, such as the types of datasets to be acquired, their sources, the need for metadata, data acquisition frequency, and volumes. In addition, look at how the datasets are to be used, such as required models, retention times, types of analyses, the types of reports, and operational integration within the business processes. Use this exercise as a model in big data architecture.
4. **Assess application platform requirements**: For the pilot, consider the hardware and software requirements for designing, building, executing, and testing the pilot—deciding the resources that are needed, determining which of the resources are available, and evaluating the options and alternatives for temporarily acquiring the components of the platform.
5. **Assess skills requirements**: Consider the need for system engineers, programmers with experience in high-performance/parallel/distributed computing, practitioners with data management skills, business intelligence developers, data integration specialists, and data scientists/analysts.
6. **Prepare the environment for the pilot**: Select, install, and configure the hardware, storage, data management, data integration, reporting/analytics, and application development components to allow for application design, development, and testing. Make sure there are

methods for measuring the performance metrics specified at the beginning of the process.

7. **Design, develop, test**: Consider algorithms and design for a selected computational model. Develop the application within a "sandbox" that allows for iterative execution, debugging, performance analysis, performance tweaking, etc. Ensure that the proper tests have been developed and that there are processes for running tests and sharing the results.

8. **Evaluate success criteria**: Continually monitor performance measures, and review scores of defined success metrics to determine if the pilot or proof of concept demonstrated measurable value and met the business users' performance objectives.

At this point, it should be clear whether the selected big data capability has the potential to add business value. Other questions remain to be answered, such as whether a production implementation is feasible, and how to go about the process of developing a reasonable plan for migration into production, or if the technology will scale from both the perspective of the user base and their anticipated performance demands. But once the go/no-go decision is made, the next step is to ensure that successful piloted technology can be migrated into the production environment.

11.6 TECHNOLOGY EVALUATION AND PRELIMINARY SELECTION

This step is intended to drive a more definitive decision regarding the evaluation of technology, and it revisits the aspects of the big data ecosystem discussed in the preceding chapters:

1. **Platform type**, specifically the type of appliance that is configured for large-scale business applications and data analytics, is often composed of multiple (typically multi-core) processing nodes connected via a high-speed network to memory and disk storage subsystems. There are two basic approaches to the platform/appliance:
   (a) **Hardware appliances** that are configured as multiprocessor systems and are designed for big data applications. They often will incorporate multiple (multi-core) processing nodes and multiple storage nodes linked via a high-speed interconnect. Support tools are usually included as well to manage high-speed

integration connectivity and enable mixed configurations of computing and storage nodes.

(b) **Software appliances** that combine a suite of high-performance software components that can be layered on commodity hardware. Software appliances can be configured to support database management software coupled with a high-performance execution engine and query optimization to best take advantage of parallelization and data distribution.

2. **Storage system**, which is used for capturing, manipulating, and analyzing massive datasets. An example is HDFS (the Hadoop Distributed File System), discussed in Chapter 7. The characteristics of a storage system that are relevant for evaluation in relation to the proposed big data application include:

(a) **Scalability**, which looks at whether expectations for performance improvement are aligned with the additional of storage resources, and the degree to which the storage subsystem can support massive data volumes of increasing size.

(b) **Extensibility**, which examines how flexible the storage system's architecture is in allowing the system to be grown without the constraint of artificial limits.

(c) **Accessibility**, which looks at any limitations or constraints in providing simultaneous access to an expanding user community without compromising performance.

(d) **Fault tolerance**, which imbues the storage environment with the capability to recover from intermittent failures.

(e) **High-speed I/O capacity**, which measures whether the input/output channels can satisfy the demanding timing requirements for absorbing, storing, and sharing large data volumes.

(f) **Integrability**, which measures how well the storage environment can be integrated into the production environment.

3. **Data management**, whose configurations may range from a traditional database management system scaled to massive parallelism to databases configured with alternative distributions and layouts, to newer graph-based or other NoSQL data management schemes. Some examples include Apache/Hadoop-related tools such as HBase, Hive, or Cassandra, or may expand to schema-less NoSQL approaches discussed in Chapter 9, such as key−value stores, document stores, tabular stores, or the graph analytics model discussed in Chapter 10.

4. **Application development and execution platform**, to enable the process of developing, executing, testing, and debugging new

application code. This framework should include programming models, development tools, program execution and scheduling, and system configuration and management capabilities. The MapReduce/YARN approach and HPCC are two alternatives discussed in Chapter 8.

As with the other decision points, the determination of the most suitable components must be made in the context of the return on the investment of time and resources. Here are some additional thoughts:

- Decide on the types of platforms and systems that are most suited to your organization's big data expectations.
- For each area of the technology, enumerate the key expectations and requirements for design, development, and implementation.
- For each area of the technology, specify the constraints, limitations, and enterprise technology standards to which any selected vendor's product must adhere.
- Identify vendors with products that are potential candidates for selection.
- Use the enumerated expectations, requirements, constraints, and limitations to down-select a smaller cadre of candidate suppliers.
- Invite the candidate vendors to demonstrate their products. Provide guidance about the types of problems to be addressed and ensure that the vendors' products can adequately be used to address those problems.
- Identify any other business-related vendor selection criteria. Assemble a weighted "scorecard" template for each vendor.
- Score the vendor products. Use the scorecards to guide the decision-making process.

11.7 APPLICATION DEVELOPMENT, TESTING, IMPLEMENTATION PROCESS

Every organization relies on certain principles and practices around application development and the system development life cycle (SDLC), and it is not the place of this book to recommend one approach over another. Rather, from a practical standpoint, here are some tasks for adapting the organization's SDLC to big data application development:

- **Environments**: Typically, an application development activity will require three core environments—one for the developers, one for testing, and one that is used in production. One of the challenges in big data application development is the "bigness"—how can you establish both a test and a production environment that can accommodate both the data volumes and expectations for computational scalability? The approach must enable testing that demonstrates the scalability of the developed application as well as enable the identification of any potential performance issues. The test environment must also be able to allow the testers and developers to duplicate any identified runtime errors discovered in production.

- **Application development**: Having chosen a preferred execution and programming model, verify that there are the proper tools for code development, including code editors, compilers, the right set of libraries, debugging tools, etc.
- **Training**: As we discussed in Chapter 8, there is often an expectation of simply installing the tools and gaining the increased performance, but in reality, there is some skill necessary to become adept at amply taking advantage of the high-performance capabilities. Therefore, it is valuable to continue to train your developers and testers in different aspects of big data.

11.8 PLATFORM AND PROJECT SCOPING

After selecting the components and products that will form the basis of your big data architecture, there are a number of decisions to be considered when assembling the development, testing, and production environments for big data application development. This largely surrounds the organization and sizing of hardware and software aspects of the platform. These decisions must be framed by a number of key variables, namely:

1. Problem data size: What volume of data is expected to be used for the analyses? Is the data both structured and unstructured? Is the data primarily transaction data? Will there be a need to augment and expand the data volumes beyond the datasets' original sizes?
2. Computational complexity: What are the types of computation that need to be performed, what are the scaling factors of the algorithms with respect to the necessary computation, and how does that compare to the volume of the data?
3. Scalability: How do the resource requirements change as either the amount of data increases, the number of applications increases, or the size of the user community grows?

4. Storage capacity configurations: How much data needs to be available in storage nodes at the same time? How much tertiary storage is required for loading and off-loading application data? How much data is required to be archived on a periodic basis? What is the duration of that period?

5. Storage hierarchy: There are different options for levels in the storage and memory hierarchy. How much computation is expected to be performed with data in-memory? How much RAM is required at each compute node? Are there benefits of using a mix of solid-state devices (SSDs) and traditional disk technologies?

6. I/O performance: How much data will be streamed into the big data environment, and at what rate? Are there optimal configurations for I/O channels and storage devices to rapidly load data into the environment? How many channels are necessary?

All of these questions can help guide the initial configurations as well as provide guidelines for expansion as any one set of variables change. This will help reduce and control the ongoing costs of development, operation, and continuous management and maintenance of the big data platform.

11.9 BIG DATA ANALYTICS INTEGRATION PLAN

Big data should not be seen as an independent "processing silo." Rather, it is important that any big data analytics applications (and their results!) be properly incorporated within the organization's general data warehousing, business intelligence, and reporting framework. Although big data will combine its own specialty aspects of hardware, data management, software, data models, and analytical models assembled with practitioner expertise, the results should be aligned with other reporting and analysis activities as well as directly integrated within the business environment. That is the best way to derive the actionable insight driving profitable business value.

Business integration goes beyond the methods discussed for soliciting requirements. Rather, asking questions such as these will highlight the business process interfaces necessary to fully integrate big data into the environment:

• Who are the participants in the process?
• What are the desired outcomes of the process?

- What information is available to the participants?
- What knowledge is provided by big data analytics?
- How are the different information assets linked together?
- How are actionable results delivered to the participants?
- What are the expectations for decisions to be made and actions to be taken?
- How are results of decisions monitored?
- What additional training and guidance are needed?
- How do business processes need to be adjusted to make best use of big data analytics?

Reviewing the answers to these questions will guide the technical teams in properly leveraging big data within the business context.

11.10 MANAGEMENT AND MAINTENANCE

Once the applications have been developed, implemented, and put into production, one additional facet to consider is ongoing management of the big data program and continuous maintenance of the platform. There are two aspects to management and maintenance. The first is the physical aspect in ensuring that the system is operating properly, that it remains properly scoped and sized, and that the performance continues to meet agreed-to levels of service.

The second aspect is organizational—continuing to identify potential opportunities to create value through the use of big data analytics, developing the processes for engaging business users, and most importantly, developing a funding model for acquisition of additional resources (including storage, compute, network, staff, and space). The ongoing program management task will oversee the key concepts discussed in this chapter, such as:

- Prioritized project plan
- Technology acquisition and integration plan
- Data integration plan
- Application development plan
- Staffing and skills management
- Business integration plan
- Training and change management

11.11 ASSESSMENT

To determine when it makes sense to invest in the effort and resource for big data, you need to know when the value created exceeds the costs of operations. More to the point, you would want to consider how to quantify potential lift and specify success criteria, as well as standardizing ways of estimating and then measuring the benefits.

Determining the degree to which big data addresses the business drivers is a function of casting the performance improvement in the context of the specific organizational business drivers discussed in Chapter 2 such as increased revenue, decreased costs, improved productivity, reduced risk, or improved customer experience, among others.

To paraphrase our discussion in Chapter 2, there are two stereotypical results of employing big data technologies: "doing things faster/cheaper" or "getting better results." The most beneficial scenarios occur when there is synergy between those two value drivers, where "faster/cheaper" leads to "better results" or where "better results" lead to "faster/cheaper." And at the point of assessment of value, quantifying the success criteria for big data necessarily involves linking "bigger," "faster," "cheaper," and/or "better" to measurable value.

These business drivers are very high level, as there may be many ways to increase revenue as well as many ways to decrease costs. The goal is to determine specific areas of the business that are served by bigger/faster/cheaper/better analysis, and then articulate specific opportunities for creating value. At that point, you can assess existing gaps in the speed or volume and throughput of existing systems and consider how the increase in volume/speed/throughput/quality of results contributes to closing those gaps.

And that becomes the key question: What is the potential lift for any one specific value driver in relation to better system performance? Investing resources in building a system with no expectation of improvement is a speculative approach that is somewhat risky. Alternatively, suggest specific value improvements to be achieved through the use of the big data analytics activity, along with improvement targets and use those as the success criteria.

11.12 SUMMARY AND CONSIDERATIONS

In this relatively short book, we have covered much about the opportunities for value creation that can be derived from a strategy for big data and big data analytics. We began by looking at the business drivers and market conditions that have enabled broad acceptance of big data analytics, including commoditization of hardware and software, increased data volumes, growing variation in types of data assets for analysis, different methods for data delivery, and increased expectations for real-time integration of analytical results into operational processes. This was followed by a discussion of the characteristics of business problems that traditionally have required resources that exceeded the enterprises' scopes, yet are suited to solutions that can take advantage of the big data platforms (either dedicated hardware or virtualized/cloud-based).

By understanding who in the organization needs to be involved in the process of acquiring, proving, and then deploying big data solutions, we considered aspects of organizational alignment, roles and responsibilities, and how people in the organization must work together to integrate big data into the system development life cycle. Further examination of some of the key issues that often plague new technology adoption suggested that the key issues are not new ones. There is likely to be organizational knowledge that can help in fleshing out a reasonable strategic plan for integrating big data into the enterprise.

We followed the discussion of a strategic plan by reviewing some of the technical aspects of big data. We first looked at the information management aspects and the need for oversight and governance for the data, especially when those developing big data applications often bypass traditional IT and data management channels. We looked at high-performance analytics appliances: specialty hardware and software designed for analytics and how they are engineered to accommodate large datasets.

The book then reviewed some common big data tools and techniques, with a high-level overview of tool suites such as Hadoop as well as methods for developing big data applications using programming models such as MapReduce and YARN. We also reviewed different approaches to data management, particularly the NoSQL alternative methods of data management that are being adopted for big data application development. We also allocated a separate chapter to another approach using graph analytics, which looked at business problems suited for graph analytics, what differentiates the problems from traditional approaches, and considerations for discovery versus search analyses.

This final chapter provided guidance about some first steps to take and ideas for fleshing out the big data strategy. However, do not feel compelled to jump alone into big data—your organization will benefit from engaging knowledgeable industry experts with experience in designing, developing, and implementing scalable high-performance business applications. There is significant value in working with these individuals to perform an assessment of the organization's readiness for big data, for laying out a blueprint of alternatives for employing big data for business value, and developing a strategic roadmap and program plan that can make big data a reality.

11.13 THOUGHT EXERCISES

As we bring the book to a close, here are some final questions to consider:

- How does your big data roadmap differ from one organized for any other emerging technology?
- Does your roadmap plan allow for alternative approaches to instantiating the big data environment? What variables are used for making the final selection?
- What measures and controls are put in place to continuously monitor the return on investment for implementing a big data environment?
- How do you plan on communicating the value of big data to your organization?
- Have you brought the right advisors and experts into your organization to best develop your big data strategy?

CPSIA information can be obtained at www.ICGtesting.com
Printed in the USA
BVOW11s2248190114

342231BV00008B/272/P